The History of Rome

CRAFTED BY SKRIUWER

Copyright © 2025 by Skriuwer.

All rights reserved. No part of this book may be used or reproduced in any form whatsoever without written permission except in the case of brief quotations in critical articles or reviews.

At **Skriuwer**, we're more than just a team—we're a global community of people who love books. In Frisian, "Skriuwer" means "writer," and that's at the heart of what we do: creating and sharing books with readers worldwide. Wherever you are in the world, **Skriuwer** is here to inspire learning.

Frisian is one of the oldest languages in Europe, closely related to English and Dutch, and is spoken by about **500,000 people** in the province of **Friesland** (Fryslân), located in the northern Netherlands. It's the second official language of the Netherlands, but like many minority languages, Frisian faces the challenge of survival in a modern, globalized world.

We're using the money we earn to promote the Frisian language.

For more information, contact : **kontakt@skriuwer.com** (www.skriuwer.com)

Disclaimer:
The images in this book are creative reinterpretations of historical scenes. While every effort was made to accurately capture the essence of the periods depicted, some illustrations may include artistic embellishments or approximations. They are intended to evoke the atmosphere and spirit of the times rather than serve as precise historical records.

TABLE OF CONTENTS

CHAPTER 1: THE LAND BEFORE ROME

- *Ancient tribes and geography shaping the future city*
- *Influences from the Latins, Etruscans, and Greek colonies*
- *Early trade routes and religious beliefs*

CHAPTER 2: THE FOUNDING LEGENDS

- *Myths of Aeneas, Romulus, and Remus*
- *Symbol of the she-wolf and the divine ancestry of Rome*
- *The Sabine women and Rome's early population growth*

CHAPTER 3: EARLY KINGS AND DAILY LIFE IN THE KINGDOM

- *Seven legendary kings ruling from the Palatine Hill*
- *Social structures, religious rituals, and family life*
- *The transition from small settlement to organized monarchy*

CHAPTER 4: THE BIRTH OF THE REPUBLIC

- *Overthrow of Tarquin the Proud and end of monarchy*
- *Creation of consuls, the Senate, and voting assemblies*
- *War with Etruscans and neighboring tribes*

CHAPTER 5: STRUGGLES OF THE EARLY REPUBLIC

- *Conflict of the Orders between patricians and plebeians*
- *Tribune of the Plebs and the Law of the Twelve Tables*
- *Constant threats from neighboring Latin states*

CHAPTER 6: EXPANSION ACROSS ITALY

- *Growth of Roman territory beyond Latium*
- *Road building and the establishment of Roman colonies*
- *Samnite Wars shaping Rome's dominance in the peninsula*

CHAPTER 7: THE WARS WITH CARTHAGE

- *First Punic War and Rome's naval innovations*
- *Hannibal's campaigns in the Second Punic War*
- *Destruction of Carthage in the Third Punic War*

CHAPTER 8: TURNING INTO A MEDITERRANEAN POWER

- *Rome's involvement in Greece and the Hellenistic kingdoms*
- *Defeat of Macedonian and Seleucid forces*
- *Creation of a provincial system in the wider Mediterranean*

CHAPTER 9: SOCIAL CHANGES AND REFORMERS

- *Rise of the Gracchi brothers and land redistribution*
- *Social War granting Italian allies citizenship*
- *Increasing class tensions and calls for reform*

CHAPTER 10: THE RISE OF STRONG GENERALS

- *Gaius Marius's army reforms and multiple consulships*
- *Sulla's dictatorship and proscriptions*
- *Pompey and Crassus's ambitions paving the way for Caesar*

CHAPTER 11: THE END OF THE REPUBLIC

- *First Triumvirate of Caesar, Pompey, and Crassus*
- *Civil War and Caesar's dictatorship*
- *Assassination of Caesar and the Second Triumvirate*

CHAPTER 12: THE AGE OF AUGUSTUS

- *Augustus's careful consolidation of power*
- *Founding of the Principate and the Pax Romana*
- *Religious, social, and political reforms shaping imperial rule*

CHAPTER 13: THE EARLY EMPERORS

- *Julio-Claudian dynasty from Tiberius to Nero*
- *Year of the Four Emperors and the rise of Vespasian*
- *Flavian rule and Domitian's authoritarian style*

CHAPTER 14: ROME'S GOLDEN AGE AND THE FIVE GOOD EMPERORS

- *Nerva's smooth transition after Domitian*
- *Trajan's conquests and Hadrian's fortified frontiers*
- *Antoninus Pius's peaceful reign and Marcus Aurelius's philosophic leadership*

CHAPTER 15: EVERYDAY LIFE IN IMPERIAL ROME

- *Social classes, family structures, and roles of slaves*
- *Housing differences between domus and insulae*
- *Baths, chariot races, gladiatorial games, and religious festivals*

CHAPTER 16: CHALLENGES AND THE CRISIS OF THE THIRD CENTURY

- *Soldier-emperors and rampant civil wars*
- *Barbarian invasions and severe economic decline*
- *Aurelian's reconquest and Diocletian's early reforms*

CHAPTER 17: REFORMS AND THE LATE EMPIRE

- *The Tetrarchy established by Diocletian*
- *Economic controls, bureaucratic expansion, and the Great Persecution*
- *Constantine's rise, Christian policies, and founding of Constantinople*

CHAPTER 18: THE SPLIT BETWEEN EAST AND WEST

- *Theodosius I's final reunion of the empire and its partition*
- *Rise of distinct Eastern (Byzantine) and Western halves*
- *Barbarian pressures and major sacks of Rome*

CHAPTER 19: THE FALL OF THE WESTERN EMPIRE

- *Visigoths, Vandals, and loss of crucial provinces*
- *Aetius, Majorian, and failed revivals under puppet emperors*
- *Deposition of Romulus Augustulus by Odoacer in AD 476*

CHAPTER 20: ROME'S LEGACY THROUGH LATE ANTIQUITY

- *Byzantine Empire carrying on Roman law and culture*
- *Spread of Latin into Romance languages and Church influence*
- *Medieval kingdoms claiming Roman heritage and ongoing global impact*

CHAPTER 1

THE LAND BEFORE ROME

Rome's story begins in a land that was wild and not yet fully explored. Before Rome became a city, ancient Italy was home to many different people and tribes. Some groups were farmers, and others were wanderers who moved with their animals. The land was full of hills, mountains, and rivers. People lived in small villages and tried to survive by hunting, fishing, or farming. This was long before big roads or large towns.

The Geography of Early Italy

Early Italy had thick forests, rolling hills, and the important Tiber River in the central region. To the north, there were tall mountains called the Alps. The Alps formed a great barrier between Italy and the rest of Europe. To the east ran the Apennine Mountains, a long chain that goes down Italy like a spine. In these early days, the people had little contact with faraway lands. They mostly stayed near their own villages.

Even so, Italy had good land for growing crops, especially near rivers and in valleys. Grapes and olives would later become very famous in Roman times, but even before Rome, local tribes were learning to grow these plants. Italy's mild climate helped them grow food for their families. Wild animals like wolves and boars roamed the forests, and the sea provided fish for those who lived near the coast.

The Peoples Before Rome

Historians believe that Italy was home to several main groups. One group we call the **Latins**, who lived in the region called Latium. This is where Rome would later appear. There were also the **Etruscans**, who were a more advanced people living north of Latium. They built strong cities and had unique art and religion. In the south of Italy, there were Greek colonies. These were people from Greece who sailed across the sea and built new towns on the coast. Because of them, this region was sometimes called **Magna Graecia**, meaning "Great Greece."

There were also groups like the Sabines, Samnites, and others who lived in more mountainous areas. Each group had its own customs, gods, and styles of clothing. There was no single ruler over all of these tribes. They often fought each other over land or resources, but they also traded goods like grains, metals, and pottery.

Early Trade and Cultural Exchange

Trade in ancient Italy usually happened by sea or along rivers. The Tiber River was especially important because it ran across central Italy. Small boats could travel on this river, carrying goods from one settlement to another. People traded salt from the salt beds near the coast, which was a valuable item used to preserve food. Salt was so important that eventually the Romans built a road named the Via Salaria, or "Salt Road." But this was in later times. For now, imagine small boats and simple paths rather than big roads.

Cultural exchange happened because tribes would meet in market areas. They would show each other new ways of making pottery or weaving cloth. Over time, skills were passed from one group to another. For example, the Etruscans were known for their metalworking and their knowledge of building techniques, such as using arches. Later, Rome would learn many of these skills from the Etruscans.

Mythology and Storytelling

Before Rome, many stories and legends were told around campfires. People believed in many gods, each linked to nature. There were gods of the sky, the sea, and the harvest. They believed that spirits lived in the rivers and forests. When storms came, they might think a spirit was angry. When the harvest was good, they thanked their gods.

Stories were passed down by word of mouth. People might explain why a hill looked a certain way or why a certain cave was sacred by telling a legend about a hero or a goddess. These stories would later blend with Roman myths. One day, these myths would shape the founding legends of Rome itself.

Etruscan Influence

Although we are focusing on the land before Rome, we must understand the Etruscans because they influenced Rome greatly. The Etruscans lived in the region called Etruria, which is roughly the area of modern Tuscany. They built walled cities on hilltops. Their tombs were decorated with colorful paintings. They had kings and priests who performed elaborate rituals.

The Etruscans traded with Greeks and Phoenicians, so they were exposed to new ideas. They adopted the Greek alphabet and changed it a bit to create their own. The Etruscans were also skilled sailors, traveling across the seas to trade. Their closeness to Rome's future location meant they would play a big role in the early history of the city.

Early Settlements Along the Tiber

The Tiber River was a vital waterway, and small settlements popped up along its banks. These were likely collections of huts where people lived in families or clans. They built walls of mud and wooden stakes, or sometimes no walls at all if the settlement was very small. They raised animals and grew simple crops like wheat or barley. Some also went hunting or gathered wild fruits and herbs.

Why did they choose the Tiber area? One reason might be the river crossing. You can only cross the Tiber easily at certain points. These places became natural spots for trade and for building a settlement. Another reason was the nearby hills. Living on top of a hill was safer because you could see enemies coming. One of these hills would eventually become the Palatine Hill, where Rome's story would begin.

Climate and Natural Challenges

The climate in central Italy was generally mild, with rainy winters and hot summers. But sometimes, there were floods that washed away crops. Fires were also a danger, since huts were often made of straw or wood. Disease could spread quickly because medicine was limited, and people did not understand germs. When droughts happened, it was hard to find enough food.

Even so, the people learned to adapt. They dug wells or built small channels to bring water from streams. They used clay pots to store grains so rodents could not get to them. Over time, these small improvements allowed settlements to grow bigger. But in these very early days, life was still quite simple.

Religious Practices and Rituals

Before Rome adopted a more formal religion, local tribes had their own rituals. They might sacrifice an animal to please a god or to ask for help with crops. They might hold festivals during certain times of the year, like planting or harvest seasons. Priests or shamans would lead the ceremonies, sometimes wearing special robes or masks. The details of these rituals are not all known today, because the people did not leave many written records.

Ancient people often looked to nature for signs. For instance, if a flock of birds flew in a special pattern, they might see that as a sign from the gods. If a lightning bolt struck a certain tree, they might think it was cursed or blessed. These beliefs would later appear in Roman culture too. The Romans would pay attention to the flights of birds and the behavior of animals to predict the future.

The First Paths of Warfare

Tribal warfare in early Italy was common. Conflicts happened over farmland, water sources, or simply the desire for more territory. Warriors used simple weapons, like spears and swords made of bronze or early iron. They wore animal skins or basic armor if they had the resources. Battles were often small-scale skirmishes, not huge organized conflicts.

When a tribe felt threatened, they might set up wooden walls or sharpened stakes around their village. If a rival tribe attacked, the defenders tried to keep them from entering. Fighting was often brutal. People had no advanced medicine to treat serious wounds, so many died if they were hurt badly.

Growing Contacts with the Wider World

Although this was the land before Rome, Italy was not fully cut off from the rest of the world. Phoenician traders from the eastern Mediterranean sometimes traveled to the western seas. Greek sailors settled on the southern coasts. These visitors brought new crafts, improved metal tools, and ideas about government or religion.

This early interaction laid the foundation for future growth. As soon as local tribes saw new ways of doing things, they might try them in their own villages. Over time, small changes added up. Potter's wheels might be introduced, improving the quality of pottery. Better methods of forging iron meant stronger weapons and farming tools. Such advancements would be very important for the rise of Rome later.

The Importance of Family and Community

For these tribes, family (or clan) was the center of everyday life. People lived in extended families: grandparents, parents, aunts, uncles, and children all together. They farmed the land as a group and shared tasks. Each member had a role. Some gathered food, some cared for animals, and others built and repaired huts.

When bigger decisions needed to be made—like going to war or moving to a new location—elders or chiefs discussed the options. Such decisions were guided by tradition and by the tribe's needs. Loyalty to one's family or tribe was a strong bond, often more important than anything else.

Changes in Material Culture

Archaeologists study pottery fragments, tools, and bones to learn about these people. They have found that over time, the style of pottery changed from simple hand-made pieces to those shaped on a potter's wheel. Decorations also grew more complex, reflecting influences from other regions.

Metal tools and weapons show that people learned about smelting and forging metals. They discovered that mixing copper with tin made bronze, which is stronger than copper alone. Later, when ironworking spread, iron weapons became more common because they were cheaper and tougher. These steps in material culture set the stage for the advanced technologies Rome would one day use.

Early Social Hierarchies

Although we do not have complete records, it seems likely that some members of these tribes had higher status. Perhaps they owned more livestock or had strong leadership qualities. These individuals could become chiefs or headmen. They might live in bigger huts or have better weapons and jewelry.

Religion could also create social hierarchy. Priests or shamans held special influence because they claimed to speak to the gods or interpret omens. People might bring them gifts in exchange for blessings or advice. As societies grew bigger, these roles would become more formal, eventually becoming the roles of kings or rulers.

Approaching the Edge of Rome's Birth

As we move closer to the time when Rome appears in history, we see how these different elements blend. The Etruscans were growing powerful in the north. Greek colonies influenced the south. The Latins, Sabines, and other tribes lived in central Italy. Each group had unique customs and resources, and they often interacted with each other.

In this setting, small communities along the Tiber River began to show signs of unity. Possibly, they decided to work together for defense or trade. This cooperation could have led to the first big steps in forming a common identity. People who lived in this area might start calling themselves "Romans" once they established a shared settlement center on one of the hills by the Tiber.

Ties to Legend

Later Roman writers, such as Livy, would talk about the earliest times of Rome in a legendary way. They described the land before Rome as a place filled with mystery, wandering heroes, and divine interventions. It is hard to know how much is true and how much is myth. But these stories played a big role in how Romans thought of their past.

They believed that gods and heroes had a hand in shaping their destiny from the very beginning. This belief gave them confidence, as if they were chosen by fate to be special. Even if the reality was more humble—just small huts and farmland—the stories gave meaning to their struggles.

A Shift from Nomads to Settlers

Before large towns, some people might have been nomadic, moving from place to place in search of grass for their animals. But with the growth of farming, more people decided to stay in one spot. They cleared land, built huts, and formed small communities. Over time, these communities would become villages and then towns.

Staying in one place also meant that people could store food, grow families, and make better tools. It paved the way for markets and the exchange of ideas. This slow shift from nomadic life to settled life was a key change that would later allow Rome to develop its famous urban culture.

The Value of Waterways

For any ancient community, water was life. In central Italy, the Tiber River was crucial. It provided water for crops and for drinking. It was also a way to travel and trade. If you lived near the Tiber, you could trade with communities downstream or even near the mouth of the river at the coast.

This advantage is one reason the early Romans would pick the site they did. The Tiber was not just a source of survival but also a path to wealth. Over time, controlling the river would help Rome expand.

Gradual Organization of Society

In the centuries leading up to the founding of Rome, societies in Italy were becoming more organized. People started making rules about property, marriage, and trade. They formed councils of elders or small gatherings of leaders. These councils might decide on punishments for stealing or set guidelines for hunting. Though still simple, these were the roots of laws and government.

Having some kind of agreed-upon rules reduced chaos and allowed for more stability. If people felt that justice existed in their community, they were more likely to stay and help it grow. These early forms of rule would shape how Rome built its own political system.

Early Burial Customs

One way to learn about these ancient tribes is by studying how they buried their dead. Some practiced cremation, burning the body and placing the ashes in urns. Others buried bodies in tombs or small graves. The items left in these graves—like pots, jewelry, or weapons—tell us about the person's status and the beliefs about the afterlife.

The Etruscans, for example, built elaborate tombs with paintings on the walls, showing scenes of daily life or ceremonies. These tombs show us how advanced and wealthy some communities became. The Latins, on the other hand, had simpler burial customs, which suggests they were less wealthy or had different beliefs about death.

Exchange of Myths and Gods

As tribes interacted, they also borrowed gods and myths from each other. Over time, the gods of different areas might blend together. A local storm god might be linked with an Etruscan or Greek god. This sharing of gods and stories would later become part of the rich Roman religion, where many deities from different places were honored.

Rome, when it did form, would be famous for adopting the gods of those it conquered or admired. This made the Roman pantheon large and diverse. But the seeds of this openness to new gods were already present in the tribes before Rome.

How We Know All This

Most of these early cultures did not leave detailed written records. So how do we know about them? Archaeologists study artifacts like pottery, tools, and remains of buildings. They also study bones to learn about diet, health, and even family relations. Sometimes they find evidence of trade, like a piece of pottery from Greece in a Latin village, showing contact between the two.

Ancient writers like Livy, Dionysius of Halicarnassus, and others wrote about Rome's beginnings much later. Their accounts mix history with legend. By comparing archaeological findings with ancient texts, historians try to piece together a more accurate story. Still, there is much we do not know for sure about this period.

Leading into the Founding of Rome

As time passed, families and villages in the area that would become Rome found themselves in a good position. They were close to the Tiber crossing, near important trade routes, and not too far from the coast. They also had hills that offered protection. Gradually, these villages grew together into a single community.

This did not happen overnight. It likely took many generations. People built common gathering places, like a marketplace or a central area where they could meet for celebrations. They might have chosen a leader who could speak for all the villages. Over time, these villages merged into an early form of a town. This is where the story of Rome's founding begins.

CHAPTER 2

THE FOUNDING LEGENDS

Rome has some of the most famous legends about its founding. These legends may not be entirely true, but they form a vital part of Roman identity. Ancient Romans believed that their city was shaped by destiny. Tales of gods, heroes, and mythical events were passed down through the generations. In this chapter, we will take a close look at these legends and explore how they shaped Roman culture.

Aeneas: The Trojan Connection

One popular story about Rome's beginnings starts with a Trojan hero named **Aeneas**. According to Greek and Roman myths, Troy was a powerful city in Asia Minor (modern-day Turkey) that was destroyed by the Greeks in a long war. Aeneas, a noble warrior, fled the burning city with a small group of survivors. Guided by the gods, he sailed across the sea.

After many hardships, Aeneas arrived in Italy. Some versions say he landed near the mouth of the Tiber River. There, he made alliances with local tribes and eventually founded a city named Lavinium, after his wife Lavinia. His son, Ascanius (also called Iulus), later founded another city called Alba Longa.

Why was this story important to the Romans? It linked them to the heroic age of Greek myth, suggesting they came from a line of brave warriors favored by the gods. Later, when Rome became an empire, the story gave them a sense of grand heritage. It also explained why Romans had cultural ties to both Italy and the broader Mediterranean world.

Alba Longa and the Kings of Old

Alba Longa was said to be a city in the Alban Hills, not far from the future site of Rome. Roman tradition holds that a line of kings ruled there, starting with Ascanius, the son of Aeneas. These kings were part of a royal family that could claim divine ancestry through the goddess Venus, who was the mother of Aeneas in the myth.

This line of kings eventually leads to **Numitor**, an important figure in the Romulus and Remus story. Numitor was the rightful king of Alba Longa, but he was overthrown by his brother, **Amulius**. This set the stage for a dramatic chain of events that would result in the founding of Rome.

Although no concrete archaeological evidence confirms these legends, the Romans believed them deeply. They would point to ruins or old temples in the Alban Hills as proof of Alba Longa's existence. Even if some details were exaggerated, the idea was that Rome's roots ran very deep in Italian soil.

Romulus and Remus: Twins of Destiny

The most famous legend about Rome's founding centers on two twin brothers: **Romulus** and **Remus**. They were said to be the sons of the god Mars and a princess named **Rhea Silvia**, who was the daughter of Numitor. When the evil Amulius took over Alba Longa, he forced Rhea Silvia to become a Vestal Virgin, meaning she was not allowed to marry or have children. He hoped this would stop her from having heirs who might challenge him.

But according to the myth, the god Mars visited Rhea Silvia, and she gave birth to the twins. Furious, Amulius ordered the babies to be thrown into the Tiber River. However, the basket carrying Romulus and Remus washed ashore near the Palatine Hill. There, a she-wolf found them and nursed them until a shepherd named **Faustulus** discovered them and took them home.

This legend shows how Romans liked to imagine their beginnings. They believed they were children of both gods and heroes. Being saved by a she-wolf was a sign of nature's blessing. Over time, many statues and images of the she-wolf nursing the babies became symbols of Rome.

Growing Up in the Hills

Romulus and Remus grew up among shepherds and became strong young men. They were natural leaders who protected the countryside from robbers. Eventually, they learned about their true heritage. They joined forces with their grandfather Numitor to overthrow Amulius and restore Numitor as king of Alba Longa.

Afterwards, they decided to build a new city near the place where they had been saved. However, the twins disagreed on which hill should be the center of the city. Romulus preferred the Palatine Hill, while Remus favored the Aventine Hill. They decided to settle the argument by looking for a sign from the gods in the flight of birds. This was called **augury**, a common way in ancient Italy to predict the will of the gods.

The Dispute Between Brothers

There are different versions of what happened next. One version says Remus saw six birds first, but Romulus saw twelve a bit later. They argued over whose sign was more important. Another version says that during the building of the city's walls, Remus mocked Romulus by jumping over the partially built wall, implying it was too low to be a good defense.

In any case, the quarrel ended tragically. Romulus killed Remus or Remus died somehow during the fight. Romulus then became the sole founder of the new city, which he named **Rome**, after himself. The date Romans later gave for this event was **753 BC**.

This part of the legend shows how seriously Romans took the idea of fate and signs from the gods. It also sets a tone that Rome was founded through struggle and conflict, even within a family. This might reflect a cultural message: Rome's success came from strength and determination, even in the face of hard choices.

The First Romans

Once Romulus established the city, the legend says he realized he needed people to live in it. He declared Rome an **asylum**, a place where outcasts and fugitives could find safety. This helped the city grow quickly, but it also meant that Rome's earliest inhabitants were not all from noble backgrounds. They were ex-slaves, runaways, and others seeking a new life.

When Romulus saw that there were few women in the new settlement, he held a festival and invited a nearby tribe called the Sabines. During the festival, the Romans carried off the Sabine women to become their wives. Some stories call this event the **Rape of the Sabine Women**, though it is usually told that Romulus promised to treat them honorably as wives, not as slaves.

This story is uncomfortable to modern readers, but it served as an important tale for Romans. It showed how Rome had to do drastic things to secure its future. Later legends say that the Sabine women themselves intervened in a war between their fathers and their husbands, pleading for peace. This helped form an alliance between Romans and Sabines, who then joined the two peoples into one community.

Roman Values in the Myths

Many Roman values can be seen in these founding legends. For instance:

- **Strength and Courage:** Romulus and Remus grew up brave, and Rome was built by strong men who could fight.
- **Piety and Respect for the Gods:** The twins tried to read the gods' will through bird signs. Romans valued such rituals.
- **Hospitality and Openness:** Rome welcomed outsiders, suggesting that being Roman was more about loyalty to the city than a certain birth.
- **Unity Through Conflict:** The alliance with the Sabines showed that even conflict could lead to a stronger union.

These values would appear again and again in Rome's history. They gave Romans a sense of identity and a reason to be proud of their city's humble and yet heroic origins.

The Symbol of the She-Wolf

One of the most enduring symbols from these legends is the **she-wolf**. Statues and images of a she-wolf nursing the twin infants can be seen in museums today. Ancient Romans placed this symbol in prominent places to remind themselves of their legendary birth. It stood for resilience, natural strength, and the protection of the gods.

Romans also used the wolf as a symbol of martial spirit. Wolves are seen as fierce pack animals that fight hard for their territory. The idea that Rome was born under the care of such an animal reminded Romans that they were descended from strong, determined ancestors.

The Role of the Gods

Mars, the god of war, was said to be the father of Romulus and Remus. This gave Rome a direct link to a powerful deity. It also explained why Romans were so good at warfare. Venus, the mother of Aeneas, was also part of Rome's divine family tree, tying the city to love and beauty. In time, other gods like Jupiter, Juno, and Minerva would become central to Roman religion.

These myths helped unite people under shared beliefs. Roman religion was not just a set of rituals; it was a part of the city's identity. Festivals, offerings, and ceremonies kept the gods happy, and the gods, in turn, protected Rome.

Historical Clues in the Myths

While much of the founding story is legend, some details hint at real events. There might have been friction between different groups living near the Tiber. Over time, they merged into a single community. There could have been a local leader who unified them. The story of the Sabine women might point to the blending of distinct tribes.

Archaeologists have found evidence of early settlements on the Palatine Hill dating back to the 8th century BC, which matches the legendary date of 753 BC for Rome's founding. Postholes from huts have been discovered, suggesting simple wooden structures. This supports the idea that the city started as a cluster of hilltop villages.

Other Versions of the Legend

Not all ancient writers told the story the same way. Some said the twins were the sons of Hercules instead of Mars. Others said the she-wolf was actually a shepherd's wife nicknamed "Lupa," since "lupa" means "she-wolf" in Latin but was also a term for a certain kind of woman. Regardless of the details, the core idea is the same: Rome was founded by abandoned twins who grew up to be heroes.

Over time, the version with Mars as the father and the she-wolf as an actual wolf became the most popular. This is the story that Roman writers like Livy repeated and that Roman art celebrated. It captured the imagination of the people, linking their city to both divine favor and human bravery.

The Early Reign of Romulus

After the founding, legend says Romulus ruled as the first King of Rome. He organized the city into different groups based on family lines. He created a council of elders called the **Senate**, made up of the heads of important families. This Senate would become a key part of Roman government in later times.

Romulus is also said to have expanded Rome's lands through wars against nearby tribes. He set up the city's first religious and legal institutions. Eventually, some stories say he disappeared in a storm or was taken up to heaven by Mars. Later Romans would honor him as a god named **Quirinus**.

It is hard to know if any of this really happened or if these stories were made up to give a sense of continuity. But for Romans, Romulus was a real figure in their history, the father of their city.

Lessons from the Founding Legends

The legends of Rome's foundation are full of drama and adventure. They also teach certain lessons that were important to the Romans:

1. **Rome's destiny is guided by the gods**: From Aeneas's journey to Romulus's signs from the birds, divine guidance is everywhere.
2. **Unity can come from conflict**: The Sabine episode shows that even after a violent act, people can come together to form one community.
3. **Valor and cunning are prized virtues**: Romulus and Remus outsmarted enemies and overcame danger. Romans valued both bravery and clever thinking.
4. **Family and heritage matter**: Being descended from heroes and gods gave Romans a sense of pride and duty to live up to those standards.

These stories formed the backbone of Roman cultural identity. Children would hear them from a young age and be inspired to honor the city's traditions. Leaders would invoke them to justify their power or to encourage the people in times of war.

The Aftermath of Romulus's Rule

We left off with Romulus becoming the first King of Rome after the death of his twin brother, Remus. According to legend, Romulus reigned for many years. The city he built started small, mostly located around the Palatine Hill. Over time, it grew to include other hills as well. The people who joined Rome were from different backgrounds—some were fugitives, some were former slaves, and some were from other tribes.

During the rule of Romulus, legends say he created the first fighting force, often called the **legio**, which is where the word "legion" comes from. This group of soldiers helped protect the young city from nearby foes. Although we do not know if this part of the story is historically accurate, it shows that Romans believed their city's military strength started with Romulus himself.

Rome also formed its first Senate under Romulus. The Senate began as a council of about one hundred men, called **patres** (which means "fathers"). These men were chosen from important families in the city. They advised Romulus and helped make decisions. Over time, this Senate would play a huge role in Roman government, especially once Rome became a republic. But in these early tales, it existed mainly as a group of elders giving guidance.

The Legend of Hersilia

Some stories mention a woman named **Hersilia**, who was a Sabine captured during the famous festival when the Roman men seized Sabine women. She supposedly married Romulus or was at least a close figure in his life. Hersilia is said to have helped make peace between the Romans and the Sabines. Later, she became a respected figure in Roman lore.

This highlights an important theme in the founding myths: Rome grew partly by uniting with other tribes, sometimes through violent acts, but also through negotiation and marriage. The idea of people from different backgrounds merging into one community was key to Rome's identity. Romans later used this story to explain why they were open to people from all over Italy and, eventually, the whole Mediterranean world.

Deification of Romulus

A curious part of Romulus's story is how it ends. In some versions, he disappears in a thunderstorm or a cloud during a military exercise. The people search for him but cannot find him. Soon after, rumors spread that he was taken to the heavens by his father, the god Mars. Romans began to worship Romulus under the name **Quirinus**, a lesser-known Roman god.

Why was this important? Because it showed that Rome's founder was seen as more than a man—he was divine. This gave the city an almost sacred origin. Later Roman leaders would sometimes compare themselves to Romulus to gain respect or to link their own rule to the city's first king. Even though we cannot confirm the truth of this story, it played a strong role in how Romans viewed their first king.

Other Early Legends Tied to Rome's Foundation

While Romulus and Remus are the most famous, Rome had a few other legendary figures linked to its earliest days:

- **Carthaginian Encounters?** Some Roman storytellers hinted that the city might have had very early dealings with seafaring peoples like the Phoenicians (the ancestors of Carthage). These tales are not confirmed, but they show how Romans loved to tie themselves to mighty places and traditions.

- **Local Heroes and Nymphs:** The land around Rome was believed to be inhabited by local gods, spirits, and nymphs who protected springs and groves. The stories of these minor deities or spirits mixed with the big legends of divine ancestors.

All these smaller legends added color to the overall story of how Rome came to be. The big message was that Rome was meant to exist, guided by gods and fate. This belief in a grand destiny would follow Romans through their entire history.

The Cultural Impact of the Founding Myths

Sense of Identity

For Romans, these stories were not just fairy tales. They were the backbone of their **identity**. Children learned them at home or in school, memorizing the heroic deeds of Romulus, Remus, and Aeneas. Young men wanted to show the same bravery or leadership that these early heroes did. Older people used the legends to remind everyone of Rome's special place in the world.

Religious Ceremonies

Certain Roman ceremonies honored parts of the founding myths. For example, an annual festival known as the **Lupercalia** may have been connected, in part, to the story of the she-wolf (Latin: lupa) that nursed Romulus and Remus. During Lupercalia, priests called Luperci would run around the city, performing rituals that people believed could bring fertility and good fortune. It was a way to remember the wolves and wild beginnings of Rome.

Political Tools

Leaders sometimes used the founding legends to support their own power. If they claimed to be related to Aeneas or Romulus, it gave them a heroic image. When Julius Caesar rose to power centuries later, he liked to remind people that his family (the Julians) descended from Iulus (also called Ascanius), the son of Aeneas. This type of claim made people see him as part of the city's divine heritage.

Early Archaeological Clues

Archaeologists have found real evidence of huts on the Palatine Hill that date back to around the 8th century BC. This lines up with the traditional date of Rome's founding in 753 BC. They also found traces of fortifications and early cemeteries. While none of these finds **prove** that Romulus and Remus were real people, they do suggest that a settlement existed there in the timeframe of the legends.

In addition, traces of a wall or boundary on the Palatine might hint that early Romans tried to protect their growing settlement. Some experts call it the "Romulean wall," though that name is more traditional than historical. Still, it shows there was an attempt at organized defense in the city's earliest stages.

Mixing Myth and History

It is important to remember that the founding of Rome was likely a **process**, not a single event. Many small settlements may have joined together over decades. People likely chose a leader who brought them under one system of rules. Over time, this leader's story could have been combined with older legends, like the twin-brothers tale, to create the famous account of Romulus and Remus.

Romans themselves understood there was a difference between legend and fact, but they did not see it as sharply as we do today. For them, the symbolic truth—that Rome was favored by the gods—mattered just as much as whether Romulus was a real person.

The Enduring Power of the Founding Legends

Even after Rome expanded across Italy, then across much of Europe, North Africa, and the Middle East, the stories of its humble birth never faded. Emperors would erect statues and monuments celebrating the she-wolf and the twins. Poets like Virgil wrote epic poems, such as the **Aeneid**, to connect Rome's present glory with its mythical Trojan past.

For many Romans, the founding myths explained why their city had such success. If you believe your ancestors were chosen by the gods, you might feel a special drive to achieve great things. That confidence can shape a culture's entire outlook. Romans carried that sense of destiny with them into battles, laws, art, and governance.

From Myth to Monarchy

As we move forward in this book, we leave the purely legendary time and enter a phase where legendary figures begin to overlap with more historical ones. After Romulus, Roman tradition speaks of six more kings who ruled the city. The stories about them still have mythical elements, but we start to see clues of real political structures, social changes, and contacts with neighboring peoples.

These kings supposedly shaped Rome's rituals, religious practices, social classes, and even built important structures like the Cloaca

Maxima (a major drainage system) and the first city walls. While we cannot confirm every detail, these tales mark the shift from **the city's birth** to **the city's growth** under a monarchy.

Linking Chapters: A Preview of the Kingdom

In the next chapter, we will focus on **the Early Kings and Daily Life in the Kingdom**. We will see how Rome, under its seven legendary kings, moved from a simple gathering of huts to a more organized community. We will explore how daily life might have looked for the average person—what they ate, how they worshiped, and how they worked. We will also touch on how these kings, from Numa Pompilius to Tarquinius Superbus, left their mark on Rome.

These next stories still contain a mix of legend and fact, but they give us a glimpse into how Rome's monarchy set the stage for future greatness. Eventually, the monarchy would fall, and Rome would become a republic. But first, let us see what happened when Rome was ruled by kings.

CHAPTER 3

EARLY KINGS AND DAILY LIFE IN THE KINGDOM

The period known as the **Roman Kingdom** is usually said to have lasted from the city's founding (traditionally 753 BC) until 509 BC, when the last king was overthrown. During this time, Rome had seven legendary kings. Each king, according to the ancient stories, contributed something important to Roman society, religion, or infrastructure. While we cannot be sure how much of these stories are true, they offer valuable insight into how Romans understood their own early development.

From Legend to Early History

We ended the last chapter with Romulus. After him, six more kings supposedly ruled Rome:

1. **Numa Pompilius**
2. **Tullus Hostilius**
3. **Ancus Marcius**
4. **Lucius Tarquinius Priscus** (Tarquin the Elder)
5. **Servius Tullius**
6. **Lucius Tarquinius Superbus** (Tarquin the Proud)

Although we call them "legendary" kings, some of their achievements are referenced so often in Roman tradition that many historians believe at least portions might be based on real events. Archaeological discoveries also hint that Rome grew in power during this period.

Numa Pompilius: The Peacemaker

After Romulus, the second king was said to be **Numa Pompilius**, a Sabine by birth. Ancient Romans described Numa as a wise and religious man who brought peace to Rome.

- **Religious Foundations:** Numa is credited with establishing many priesthoods and religious orders, such as the **Flamines** (priests serving specific gods) and the **Vestal Virgins** (priestesses of the goddess Vesta). He also created the **Pontifex Maximus**, the chief priest who supervised Rome's religious life.
- **Temple Building:** Some stories say Numa built temples or introduced worship of certain gods, like Terminus (god of boundaries) and Janus (god of beginnings and endings).
- **The Roman Calendar:** Many sources say Numa adjusted the Roman calendar to align the months with lunar cycles. While details are murky, Romans credited him with improving how they measured time.

Even if these details are partly myth, they highlight the importance Romans placed on religion and order. Having a structured religious system helped unite people and set moral guidelines. It also gave the king a sacred aspect—if the king was close to the gods, people believed he should be respected.

Tullus Hostilius: The Warrior King

The third king was **Tullus Hostilius**, nearly the opposite of Numa. He was described as aggressive, eager to expand Rome's territory, and less focused on religion. According to legend:

- **The Destruction of Alba Longa:** Tullus fought against Alba Longa, the city from which Romulus's grandfather had come. The stories say Rome defeated Alba Longa and then forced the people of Alba Longa to move to Rome, doubling the city's population.
- **Warrior Culture:** Tullus was said to value martial strength. Under him, the city might have built stronger fortifications. He also brought in more arms and organized the army further.

- **Death by Lightning?** Ancient stories claim Tullus offended the gods by not performing the proper rites. In one dramatic tale, Jupiter struck him and his household with lightning.

Whether or not he really died by lightning, these stories again emphasize that Roman kings needed to respect the gods. No matter how strong Rome became in war, it had to maintain favor with divine powers.

Ancus Marcius: Balancing Peace and War

Ancus Marcius, the fourth king, was said to combine the qualities of Numa (peaceful, religious) and Tullus (warlike, ambitious). His legend includes:

- **Bridge Building:** Some accounts say Ancus built the **Pons Sublicius**, the first wooden bridge over the Tiber River. This would have been a major step in linking different parts of Rome's territory.
- **Expansion:** He reportedly founded a port at **Ostia**, near the mouth of the Tiber, to increase trade and secure salt supplies.
- **Settlement Growth:** By mixing religion, diplomacy, and conquest, Ancus was credited with bringing more people into Rome and further shaping the city's identity.

Ancus Marcius's reign suggests that Rome was not just a band of warriors but also a growing urban center interested in trade, infrastructure, and stable institutions.

Lucius Tarquinius Priscus (Tarquin the Elder)

The fifth king, **Lucius Tarquinius Priscus**, was said to be of Etruscan descent. This is important because the **Etruscans** were a major influence on early Rome. They lived to the north of the city and were known for their advanced culture, architecture, and religious practices.

- **Rise to Power:** Stories say Tarquinius Priscus moved to Rome to seek his fortune. He gained favor with Ancus Marcius, became guardian to Ancus's children, and later took the throne himself.
- **Public Works:** He is credited with constructing important works, such as the **Cloaca Maxima**, a massive drainage system that helped clear the marshy valleys between the hills. This made the city healthier and allowed for the building of the Roman Forum, the central marketplace and public space.
- **The Circus Maximus:** Tarquinius Priscus is often connected with establishing the Circus Maximus, where Romans later held chariot races and big public games.
- **Etruscan Influence:** By tradition, he brought Etruscan artisans and craftsmen to Rome, introducing the Romans to advanced metalworking, architecture, and religious customs.

The story of Tarquinius Priscus underlines how Rome, even in its early days, was open to newcomers with talent. It also shows how Etruscan ideas may have blended with Roman traditions to create something new.

Servius Tullius: The Reformer

Servius Tullius was the sixth king. His origin story is dramatic—legend says he was born a slave or of humble birth, and that a ring of fire once appeared around his head as a child, signifying he was chosen by the gods.

- **Social Organization:** Servius is credited with creating the **Servian Constitution**, dividing Roman citizens into classes based on wealth. This established a new way of organizing the army and voting. Wealthier citizens had more responsibility but also more influence.

- **City Walls:** He supposedly built or improved the **Servian Walls**, fortifying Rome's hills to protect the growing population.
- **Focus on the People:** Servius was seen as a king who cared about ordinary people. He tried to give them a voice in public decisions by setting up assemblies where citizens voted.

Though we cannot confirm every detail, Romans believed Servius laid the groundwork for how their society would function for centuries. The idea that power in Rome was partly based on a citizen's wealth or property would influence the Roman Republic as well.

Lucius Tarquinius Superbus (Tarquin the Proud)

The seventh and final king was **Lucius Tarquinius Superbus**. His nickname, "Superbus," means "proud" or "arrogant." He was the son (or possibly grandson) of Tarquinius Priscus and is remembered mostly for his harsh rule.

- **Tyrannical Behavior:** Tarquin the Proud is said to have used violence and fear to keep power. He bypassed the Senate, made decisions on his own, and crushed anyone who opposed him.
- **Building Projects:** He completed some major buildings, such as the Temple of Jupiter on the Capitoline Hill, but he did so by forcing common people to work like slaves.
- **The Fall of the Monarchy:** According to tradition, Tarquin's son committed a terrible crime against a noblewoman named **Lucretia**. Her tragic story led to a revolt against the Tarquin family. In 509 BC, the Romans expelled the king and set up a republic, vowing never again to have a king rule over them.

This final legend shows how Romans believed their kingdom ended. The monarchy period concluded in scandal and outrage, paving the way for the **Roman Republic**. We will explore the Republic in Chapter 4, but first, let us look more closely at how life might have been for everyday people during the kingdom era.

Daily Life Under the Kings

Even though much of what we know is wrapped in legends, archaeology and later Roman writings give us some hints about **daily life** in the kingdom period. Let us see how common people lived, worked, ate, and worshiped in those times.

Housing and City Layout

- **Huts to Houses:** Early Rome consisted of simple huts made from **wattle and daub** (woven wooden strips covered with clay and straw). Over time, wealthier families might have built sturdier homes using stone foundations and tiled roofs, especially when Etruscan influence increased.
- **Forum and Public Areas:** The area between the Palatine Hill and the Capitoline Hill was drained by the Cloaca Maxima, turning marshy land into the Roman Forum. The Forum became a place for markets, public speeches, and religious ceremonies.
- **Streets and Infrastructure:** Paths connecting hills gradually became more defined. Wooden bridges crossed the Tiber. While the city was not as grand as it would become later, it was already a hub of activity.

Work and Economy

- **Farming:** Most people in early Rome likely worked the land. They grew grains like wheat and barley, along with vegetables and fruits. They also kept animals such as pigs, sheep, and cattle.

- **Trade:** As Rome expanded, it controlled more trade routes. Salt from the coast was important, and the Tiber River allowed goods to move in and out. Markets in the Forum would sell pottery, metal tools, and clothing.
- **Craftsmen and Artisans:** Skilled workers made items like pottery, weapons, shields, and simple jewelry. The influence of Etruscan craftsmen introduced more advanced metalwork and pottery styles. Some artisans also built or decorated temples.

Family and Social Structure

- **Paterfamilias:** In Roman families, the oldest male, called the **paterfamilias**, held great power. He could make decisions for the whole household, arrange marriages, and manage property.
- **Roles of Women:** Women were expected to run the household, cook, and weave cloth. Some women from wealthier families had slaves to help them. While they did not have many legal rights under the monarchy, some, like Tanaquil (the wife of Tarquinius Priscus), are said to have wielded influence behind the scenes.
- **Slavery:** Slaves were present even in early Rome. They could be war captives or people who sold themselves into slavery due to debt. They usually did household chores or worked in fields.

Clothing and Appearance

- **Simple Garments:** Many Romans wore a **tunic**, a simple, knee-length garment made of wool or linen. Wealthier citizens might have longer tunics of finer material.
- **Togas for Important Men:** The **toga** was a large piece of cloth draped over the body and was worn by Roman men during public or formal occasions. However, in the kingdom period, the toga was probably less common or simpler in style than in later republic or imperial times.

- **Jewelry and Accessories**: People wore minimal jewelry—perhaps a simple necklace or ring. Women, especially from better-off families, might have hairpins or small ornaments influenced by Etruscan or Greek styles.

Food and Diet

- **Staple Foods**: Bread made from wheat or barley was a main part of the diet. Porridge was also common. People ate vegetables like onions, garlic, and beans.
- **Meat and Fish**: Meat was less common because animals were valuable for labor and milk. However, during festivals or sacrifices, people ate beef, pork, or lamb. Fish was available along the Tiber or from the coast.
- **Wine and Water**: Early Romans drank **wine** mixed with water. Pure water came from wells or the Tiber, though it was not always clean.
- **Olives and Olive Oil**: While we do not know how widespread olive cultivation was during the monarchy, olives and olive oil eventually became central to Roman cooking.

Religion and Rituals

Religion was woven into every part of daily life. People believed the gods watched over their homes, farms, and public spaces.

- **Household Gods**: Families worshiped small household gods called **Lares** and **Penates**. They might keep a tiny shrine in the home with small statues or tokens. Each day, they would offer a bit of food or wine to keep the spirits happy.
- **State Religion**: Public ceremonies honored major gods like Jupiter, Juno, and Minerva. Priests performed sacrifices at altars, offering animals, wine, or incense.

- **Festivals:** The kings are said to have introduced yearly festivals to honor the gods. These were times for the community to come together in feasts, games, and prayers.
- **Omens and Augury:** Interpreting signs from birds or natural events was common. Before important decisions—such as going to war—priests studied bird flights or animal entrails to see if the gods approved.

Entertainment

- **Games and Sports:** The early Romans enjoyed athletic contests, possibly influenced by the Etruscans and Greeks. Wrestling, running, and boxing could be part of festivals.
- **Public Gatherings:** The Circus Maximus might have begun in a simple form, hosting chariot races or horse races. Later, it became the grand stadium many people imagine.
- **Music and Dancing:** People used simple instruments like pipes, drums, or lyres. Dancing could be part of religious festivals.
- **Storytelling:** With little written literature at this stage, storytelling was a major form of entertainment. Bards or elders told tales of heroes, the gods, and the city's founding.

Rome's Interaction with Neighbors

During the monarchy, Rome did not exist in isolation. It interacted with the **Etruscans** to the north, Latin tribes in surrounding areas, and Greek colonies in southern Italy.

- **Trade Networks:** Rome's position on the Tiber River gave it an advantage for trade, letting it bring in goods from inland areas and from the coast.
- **Cultural Exchange:** The Etruscans influenced Rome's architecture (arches, drainage, temple design), religious

rituals, and possibly the style of the Roman toga. Greek colonies influenced art, pottery, and mythology.
- **Military Conflicts:** Kings like Tullus Hostilius and Ancus Marcius led campaigns against neighboring towns. Victory often meant taking prisoners who became slaves, or forcing defeated peoples to merge into Rome.

Class Divisions and the Seeds of Change

By the later monarchy, Roman society was becoming more divided between **patricians** (wealthy noble families) and **plebeians** (commoners). Patricians often claimed ancestry from the founding fathers (the Senate members chosen by Romulus). They held most of the power in government and religious offices. Plebeians, on the other hand, were the majority but had fewer legal rights and less influence.

This divide set the stage for conflicts that would grow more serious in the Republic era. Even in the kingdom, there might have been tensions over land, debt, and political power. However, since the kings often played a mediating role, the real clashes between patricians and plebeians would break out strongly only after the monarchy ended.

The Downfall of the Monarchy

As we learned, the monarchy ended when the seventh king, Tarquin the Proud, was expelled. The story focuses on the crime committed by his son against Lucretia. This sparked outrage among noble families, who saw Tarquin's rule as cruel and disrespectful of tradition. A nobleman named **Lucius Junius Brutus** led a revolt, and the people agreed to banish Tarquin.

With Tarquin gone, the Romans decided they would never again allow a single person to hold so much power. They replaced the kingship with two elected leaders called **consuls**, starting what we now call the **Roman Republic**. But before we move on to that next era, let us pause and reflect on what the monarchy achieved and how it shaped Rome.

Achievements of the Roman Kingdom

1. **Urban Development:** Rome began as a cluster of huts but grew into a walled city with public spaces, temples, and a drainage system.
2. **Religious Institutions:** Many priesthoods, festivals, and temples were credited to the early kings, setting up the deep connection between religion and state in Rome.
3. **Military Organization:** Early kings formed the basis of what would become one of history's most famous armies.
4. **Social Structures:** Systems of class division and property-based voting were established, which would heavily influence the Republic.
5. **Cultural Mix:** The kingdom period showcased Rome's openness to outside influences, especially from the Etruscans, and laid the groundwork for future expansion and adaptation.

The Lives of Ordinary People

For ordinary Romans, life under the monarchy was probably a mix of farming, religious practice, and dealing with the occasional burden of warfare or forced labor. Most would never meet the king face to face. Instead, they knew local priests, clan leaders, and perhaps soldiers enforcing royal decrees. Their main concerns were feeding their families, honoring the gods, and staying safe during conflicts.

Yet these common folks were the backbone of the city. They farmed the land, built roads and buildings, and filled the ranks of the army. Over time, they would push for more rights and representation, helping shape the republic and even the empire that followed.

The Influence of the Etruscans

It is worth emphasizing once more how much Rome owed to the Etruscans. Scholars believe that the Etruscans introduced:

- **The Arch:** Romans would later use arches in their famous aqueducts and buildings.
- **Religious Rituals:** Many rites, especially those involving reading omens from animal livers, came from Etruscan tradition.
- **Art and Craftsmanship:** Etruscan metalwork, pottery, and sculpture styles can be seen in early Roman art.
- **Urban Planning:** The Etruscans understood drainage, road-building, and fortifications, all of which helped Rome grow.

Without Etruscan input, Rome might have developed more slowly. Their guidance and rivalry pushed the city to strengthen its defenses, refine its architecture, and adopt more complex religious ceremonies.

Transition to the Republic

As we move to Chapter 4, we will see how Rome's decision to abolish the monarchy changed everything. The monarchy laid the groundwork—streets, temples, laws, class structures—but the real story of Rome's rise to dominance begins with its new form of government, the Republic.

From 509 BC onward, Rome would be led by elected officials, such as consuls and senators. This change was not sudden or perfect. There were still power struggles, and the patricians often held the most authority. Over the years, the common people (plebeians) would fight for more rights, leading to key reforms. These developments were all shaped by what happened during the kingdom period.

CHAPTER 4

THE BIRTH OF THE REPUBLIC

Setting the Stage

When we left off in the last chapter, Rome had just expelled its seventh king, **Lucius Tarquinius Superbus** (Tarquin the Proud). The Romans were angry at his harsh rule and the crime his son committed against the noblewoman **Lucretia**. In 509 BC, Roman nobles—led by **Lucius Junius Brutus**—revolted. They declared that **no king** would ever rule Rome again. Instead, they set up a new government that we now call the **Roman Republic**.

The word "republic" comes from the Latin term *res publica*, meaning "public matter" or "the public thing." Under this new system, the highest officials were **two consuls** (rather than one king). These consuls were elected by Roman citizens for a one-year term, and they could veto each other's actions. By dividing power between two men, the Romans hoped to avoid giving too much control to any single person. They also created other offices, councils, and assemblies to manage affairs.

But the path to a stable republic was not smooth. In its early years, Rome faced threats from outside, especially from the exiled Tarquin's allies. Inside the city, tensions arose between the **patricians** (wealthy families) and the **plebeians** (common people). Even so, the foundation laid in 509 BC would shape Rome for centuries. This chapter will look at how the Republic formed, who the key players were, and how early Rome managed to survive and grow under this new system.

The Expulsion of the Tarquins

The Revolt Against Tarquin the Proud

Tarquin the Proud was known for ignoring the Senate, forcing people to do heavy labor on his construction projects, and punishing anyone who spoke against him. But the event that truly ended the monarchy was the attack on Lucretia by Tarquin's son, **Sextus Tarquinius**. Lucretia was a virtuous Roman noblewoman, and she chose to end her own life out of shame and despair after this crime.

Her father and husband, together with their friend **Lucius Junius Brutus**, showed Lucretia's body to the Roman people, stirring enormous anger. They rallied support to drive out the Tarquin family. Tarquin the Proud fled with his wife and sons, seeking refuge in neighboring lands. Meanwhile, the Romans vowed never again to let a king rule them.

Swearing an Oath of Freedom

Stories say that Brutus had everyone gather, and they swore an oath that no one in Rome would ever allow the return of a king. If anyone tried to bring the Tarquins back, the Roman people would stand against them. This act created a shared sense of purpose. The Romans felt they were now free citizens rather than subjects of a cruel monarch.

They chose Brutus and another man, **Lucius Tarquinius Collatinus** (Lucretia's husband), as the first **consuls**. The consul was a brand-new position, replacing the king. Instead of ruling for life, consuls served only for one year. This change was meant to stop anyone from becoming too powerful. After a year, two new consuls (or sometimes the same men, if re-elected in later years) would replace them.

The Shape of the New Government

Consuls

The **consuls** held the highest executive power. They led the army, performed certain religious duties, and proposed laws. Both consuls had to agree on major decisions. If one consul vetoed ("I forbid") the other, the action could not proceed. This system forced them to cooperate or find compromise.

The Senate

The **Senate** continued from the time of the kings, but its role changed. It became an advisory council made up of noblemen (mostly patricians) who offered guidance to the consuls. Over time, the Senate grew very influential, handling foreign policy, finances, and more. In the early republic, senators served for life once appointed, although they could be removed for improper behavior by certain officials.

Popular Assemblies

The Romans also had **assemblies** where citizens voted on laws, elected magistrates, and made important decisions. Only free male Roman citizens could participate, and originally, many voting powers were skewed to favor the wealthy. Still, the assemblies gave ordinary citizens a chance—however limited—to have a say in Roman affairs.

Other Officials

Over time, the Romans created other offices:

- **Praetors** to help the consuls, especially with legal matters.
- **Quaestors** to handle financial duties.
- **Aediles** to oversee the city's day-to-day matters, like food supply and public buildings.
- **Censors** to count the population, manage citizenship rolls, and sometimes remove unworthy senators.

But these offices developed gradually. In the earliest days of the Republic, the main leaders were the consuls and the Senate.

Lucius Junius Brutus and the Founding Spirit

Lucius Junius Brutus was viewed as a champion of liberty. He was known for his stern sense of duty to Rome. In one famous story, his own sons joined a plot to bring back the Tarquins. Brutus discovered the plan and, despite his heartbreak, ordered his sons to be executed along with the other conspirators. This harsh action showed how Romans valued loyalty to the state above even family ties.

Though we cannot confirm the truth of every detail, Brutus symbolizes the strict dedication to the republic's principles. For Romans, the message was clear: if you tried to destroy the republic, you would face severe punishment—even if you were the consul's own son.

Early Threats to the Republic

Tarquin's Attempts to Regain Power

Once expelled, Tarquin the Proud did not just give up. He sought help from powerful neighbors. One ally was **Lars Porsenna**, the king of the Etruscan city of Clusium. According to Roman tales, Porsenna marched on Rome, hoping to restore Tarquin to the throne or at least profit from the chaos.

This led to famous stories of Roman bravery:

- **Horatius Cocles at the Bridge:** As Porsenna's army approached, the Romans tried to destroy the wooden bridge over the Tiber (the **Pons Sublicius**) so the enemy could not cross. A soldier named **Horatius Cocles** stayed behind to hold off the attackers. He fought fiercely on the narrow bridge, giving the Romans time to demolish it. Then he prayed to the river god and jumped into the Tiber, swimming back to safety.
- **Mucius Scaevola:** Another legend tells of a young Roman named **Gaius Mucius** who sneaked into the Etruscan camp to kill Porsenna. By mistake, he killed the king's scribe instead. Captured, he told Porsenna that many Roman youths had sworn to assassinate him. To prove his courage, Mucius thrust his right hand into a fire without flinching. Impressed, Porsenna released him. Mucius earned the nickname *Scaevola* (left-handed), and Porsenna supposedly ended the siege because he feared such brave Romans.

These heroic tales may be partly myth, but they show how Romans liked to see themselves: fearless, dedicated, and willing to sacrifice for their city. In some accounts, Porsenna briefly ruled Rome or forced it to make concessions, but eventually he withdrew. Tarquin the Proud, however, never regained his throne.

Battles with Etruscans and Latin Neighbors

Rome also had conflicts with other cities in Latium (the region around Rome) and with the Etruscans in the north. The Etruscans were more powerful and had strong, fortified cities. Rome's early republic had to fight hard to hold its ground. Over the next century, Romans slowly grew stronger, building alliances or sometimes forcing submission from nearby towns. This set the stage for the eventual unification of all of Latium under Rome's leadership.

Building the Foundations of Republican Power

Laws and Customs

In the early republic, Rome did not yet have a written code of laws. Instead, many customs were passed down orally or came from old royal decrees. This sometimes led to confusion or unfair treatment, especially for commoners. Over time, the Romans realized that a written set of laws would help solve disagreements, but that development (the **Law of the Twelve Tables**) would come later. For now, the early republic relied heavily on tradition and the judgments of patrician leaders.

Religious Continuity

Many of the religious practices from the monarchy continued. The consuls performed some priestly roles, and the old temples remained in use. Romans believed the gods had helped them remove the kings, so they were eager to keep the gods' favor. They still carried out sacrifices, festivals, and auguries (reading omens from birds) before major actions like battles or elections.

Diplomacy and Alliances

To protect themselves, the Romans created or joined alliances with neighboring Latin cities. They sometimes allowed defeated peoples to keep their own local customs if they agreed to be loyal allies, provide soldiers for the Roman army, and not rebel. This flexible approach to conquered or allied cities would later become a hallmark of Roman expansion. But in these early days, it was simply about survival.

Life in the Early Republic

We have already looked at daily life under the kings, but how did it change now that Rome was a republic? In many ways, ordinary people still lived, worked, and worshiped as they did before. However, the shift away from a single monarch did bring some changes over time:

- **Greater Public Involvement:** Citizens (at least male citizens) could vote for consuls and other officials. Though the wealthy had more influence, the idea of choosing leaders was new.
- **Patricians in Charge:** The patricians continued to dominate the government. They held the consulships, made key decisions in the Senate, and benefited from social rules that kept power in their hands.
- **Plebeian Discontent:** Commoners (plebeians) found they had fewer legal protections. Over the next few decades, they would protest and demand a voice in government. This conflict would shape much of the early Republic.

The Role of the Army

Citizen-Soldiers

Under the republic, Rome continued the tradition of a citizen army. Wealthier citizens served as cavalry or heavily armed infantry, while poorer citizens might serve as light infantry or skirmishers. Each year, consuls would gather eligible men for the army, especially if a campaign was planned against neighboring cities.

Military Organization

Though still developing, the Roman army began to reflect the republican spirit of shared duty. Soldiers elected their centurions (junior officers) or at least had some say in the selection. Loyalty to the republic became a strong motivator. Later on, this sense of duty would become one of the reasons for Rome's great success in warfare and expansion.

Key Early Conflicts

1. **War with the Etruscan Cities:** Rome struggled against powerful Etruscan neighbors like Veii and Tarquinii. Victories were not guaranteed, but each success boosted Roman confidence.
2. **Latin Wars:** Rome also fought or allied with other Latin towns such as Tusculum, Praeneste, and others. A mix of diplomacy and war led to the **Latin League**, a loose alliance system.
3. **Uncertain Borders:** Early Romans constantly worried about raids by hill tribes like the Volsci, Aequi, and Sabines, requiring frequent military campaigns to defend farmland and roads.

Developing Civic Pride

Even though life was hard, the idea of a republic where leaders were chosen each year gave many Romans a new sense of pride. The monarchy was associated with tyranny and cruelty—especially the last king. By contrast, the young republic represented freedom, at least for citizens who could vote and hold office. Public speeches and assemblies became occasions to boast of Rome's achievements or criticize politicians. This sense of open debate, limited though it was, laid a foundation for Roman political culture.

The Myth vs. Reality Divide

It is important to remember that many of these early stories come from writers who lived hundreds of years after the events. These authors, like Livy, wanted to show the courage and virtue of their ancestors. Some tales, like Horatius Cocles or Mucius Scaevola, might be partly or mostly legend. But they reflect how Romans viewed themselves: brave, loyal, and guided by fate to become great.

From an archaeological point of view, we see that Rome did expand slowly. Evidence of early walls, temples, and roads show an evolving city. Weapons and gravesites indicate a population prepared for regular warfare. While we may never confirm each heroic deed, the general outline—that Rome abolished monarchy, established consuls, and defended itself against neighbors—seems consistent with known history.

Consolidating the Republic

After the dramatic events of 509 BC, the Roman Republic needed to consolidate (or firm up) its new system. There was no blueprint for how to run a society without a king. The Romans improvised, guided by tradition and the collective wisdom of the Senate.

Annual Consulships

One of the most revolutionary ideas was having **two consuls** serve for **one year**. Each consul had imperium (the power to command) but could be checked by the other consul's veto. At the year's end, the consuls stepped down, and new ones were elected. This system made sure power kept moving. It also allowed Rome to adapt to changing needs. If a consul performed poorly, he would be gone when his term ended.

But the early consuls were nearly all **patricians**. This meant that the richest families effectively rotated power among themselves. Plebeians had no direct path to the consulship at first. They could vote in assemblies but could not hold the highest office. This inequality caused resentment, leading eventually to the **Conflict of the Orders** (which we will see more of in Chapter 5).

The Senate's Growing Influence

With no king, the Senate took on greater importance. It advised consuls on decisions about war, treaties, and finances. Technically, the Senate could not pass laws on its own, but its recommendations (senatus consulta) were very influential. Over time, the Senate became the chief guiding body of the Republic, a place where experienced politicians debated the city's future.

Civic Duty

Romans began to develop a strong sense of **civic duty**. Wealthy citizens were expected to serve in public office, lead armies, or fund public works. Even though they often benefited from power, they were also expected to do what was best for the city. This sense of responsibility was not always followed perfectly, but the ideal was admired. In time, men who served the Republic faithfully gained honor and prestige.

Social and Economic Life

Farms and Land Ownership

Most of Rome's wealth at this time came from **agriculture**. Owning farmland was key to a family's status. After wars, Romans might seize land from defeated neighbors and distribute it among patricians or wealthy plebeians. This process would become a source of tension because land was limited, and poorer citizens felt left out of these distributions.

Trade and Crafts

The Tiber River and roads connecting Rome to nearby towns helped **trade** grow. Artisans made pottery, tools, and textiles. Some Romans traveled to Etruscan cities or Greek colonies in southern Italy to buy and sell goods. Though small by later standards, this trade network boosted Rome's economy and gave it resources to maintain a steady supply of weapons and everyday goods.

Slavery Expands

Warfare produced **slaves**, either captured in battle or sold by enemies. Slave labor became more common in fields, workshops, and homes. While slaves had no rights, it was possible—though rare—for a trusted slave to be freed, becoming a freedman who owed loyalty to the former master. This system of slavery would grow over time, becoming a defining feature of Roman society.

Daily Life for Plebeians

For the average plebeian family, life was still modest. They lived in simple homes, ate basic meals of bread, porridge, and vegetables. Some might own a small piece of land or work as laborers for richer landowners. There were no big differences yet between the rich and the super-rich, but over time, patricians would accumulate more wealth, and the gap between classes widened.

Military Structure and Campaigns
Annual Military Campaigns

Every year in the spring, the consuls—if war was on the agenda—would muster the Roman army. Campaigns usually lasted until autumn, when soldiers needed to return home to harvest crops. Romans fought short, sharp wars against nearby tribes, seizing territory or forcing alliances. This pattern repeated year after year, allowing Rome to expand step by step.

Citizen Soldiers

Roman soldiers were primarily **citizen-farmers**, not professional warriors. They fought for a season, then went back to their farms or trades. This arrangement worked as long as campaigns did not drag on too long. It also meant the army had a strong sense of camaraderie, since soldiers felt they were defending their own lands and families.

Role of Cavalry

Wealthier citizens who could afford a horse served in the **cavalry**. They had higher status and usually came from patrician families or well-off plebeian families. Cavalry units were smaller in number but played important roles in scouting and flanking maneuvers during battles.

External Challenges

Ongoing Etruscan Threat

The Etruscans to the north remained a formidable foe. Cities like **Veii** were close to Rome—only about 16 kilometers (10 miles) away. Frequent conflicts erupted over farmland, trade routes, or political influence. Romans learned much from fighting the Etruscans, including siege tactics, which they would use later on in bigger conquests.

Rival Latin Cities

Not all Latin cities wanted Rome to dominate. Some joined alliances against Rome, others made peace treaties. Over time, Rome worked to become the leading power in Latium. These local struggles kept the early Republic busy, but they also honed the Romans' military and diplomatic skills.

Mountain Tribes

The **Sabines**, **Aequi**, and **Volsci** were tribes living in the hilly or mountainous areas east and southeast of Rome. They often raided Roman territory or that of Roman allies. The consuls frequently led armies against these tribes to push them back or take their lands. These repeated skirmishes played a large part in early Roman military history.

The First Steps Toward Class Conflict

As the Republic took shape, the main struggle inside Rome was between the **patricians** (aristocrats) and the **plebeians** (commoners). This brewing conflict would eventually lead to significant reforms:

1. **Economic Hardship for Plebeians:** Frequent wars meant plebeian farmers might see their lands damaged or have a hard time paying debts. If they failed to pay, they could become debt-bonded servants or lose their property.
2. **Lack of Political Representation:** Plebeians had votes in assemblies but had no chance to become consuls or hold the highest offices. The government was firmly in patrician hands.
3. **Legal Inequality:** Without written laws, patrician judges could interpret rules in favor of themselves and their allies. Plebeians felt they had no fair recourse in disputes.

These issues would not explode into major reforms until later, but the seeds were planted. As the Republic gained stability and faced new challenges, plebeian voices grew louder, demanding a fairer share in Rome's success.

Notable Early Consuls and Events

Over the first few decades of the Republic, some noteworthy individuals and incidents stand out:

- **Publius Valerius Publicola ("Poplicola"):** An early consul known for passing laws that favored the people, such as reducing harsh punishments. He was admired for living modestly and respecting the will of the citizens.
- **The Battle of Lake Regillus (c. 496 BC):** A legendary victory of Rome over a coalition of Latin cities, sometimes said to have been aided by the gods Castor and Pollux. This battle, if real, helped secure Roman influence in Latium.
- **Temple Building:** Early consuls sponsored the construction of temples to gods like Saturn, Castor, and Pollux, marking victories and dedicating them to divine powers.

Stories about these consuls and events reminded Romans of the Republic's formative ideals: courage, piety, and service to the community.

Religion and the Early Republic

Romans believed that the gods had helped rid them of the last king. Therefore, they kept up with **regular sacrifices**, festivals, and rituals to maintain divine favor. Temples built during these years served as public statements that the Republic was under the gods' protection.

Some roles previously held by the king were reassigned to certain priests or to the consuls themselves. For example, the **Rex Sacrorum** (King of Sacrifices) was a priestly role that performed some religious tasks the kings had once done, but without having any political power. This was another way to ensure that no single person ever had the authority of a king again.

Growth of the Forum

The **Roman Forum**, which started coming together in the late monarchy, became the heart of the city under the Republic. People gathered there for markets, political speeches, and trials. Important buildings, such as the **Curia** (Senate House) and various temples, lined the edges. Over time, the Forum would gain more structures like basilicas (public halls) and commemorative monuments.

As the city expanded, Romans also constructed new roads, bridges, and defensive walls. Although these might seem like small improvements, they were essential for uniting the population and keeping out enemies.

Moral Lessons from Early Republic Legends

Romans of later centuries looked back on this time as a golden era of virtue. They loved telling stories that highlighted the moral code of the early Republic:

- **Obedience to Law:** People like Brutus even punished their own sons if they conspired against the Republic.
- **Honor in War:** Heroes like Horatius Cocles and Mucius Scaevola risked their lives for the city.
- **Simplicity and Duty:** Consuls, like Publicola, were praised for not living in luxury and for listening to the citizens.

Though the reality may have been more complicated, these legends shaped how future Romans saw themselves and guided how they believed a good Roman should behave.

The Seeds of Rome's Future Greatness

By the end of the 6th century BC and moving through the 5th century BC, Rome was still a small city compared to places like Carthage or the Greek cities in southern Italy. However, the Republic's structures, values, and army organization set it apart from many neighbors. Key foundations included:

1. **Rotation of Power:** Annual consulships kept fresh leadership and prevented tyranny.
2. **Citizen Participation:** Even if incomplete, voting assemblies gave Roman citizens a role in choosing leaders and passing laws.
3. **Flexible Diplomacy:** Rome allied with some cities, fought others, and learned to incorporate new ideas from different cultures.
4. **Stubborn Defense:** The stories of Horatius and Mucius point to a fierce will to fight for independence.

These traits would prove vital as Rome continued to grow. Over the next centuries, Rome would face challenges, adapt, and refine its republican system. By learning from early mistakes, the Romans gradually built a powerful network of alliances and a strong internal government.

Looking Ahead to Chapter 5

We have seen how the Roman Republic began, survived the first threats from the exiled king and the Etruscans, and started organizing its society around new principles. However, all was not peaceful. Class tensions were rising, and plebeians started to protest their lack of rights. In **Chapter 5: Struggles of the Early Republic**, we will explore:

- The **Conflict of the Orders** between patricians and plebeians.
- How plebeians forced political change through actions like the **Secession of the Plebs**.
- The creation of the **Tribunes of the Plebs** and the **Law of the Twelve Tables**, which began the process of giving commoners some protection under the law.
- Continued wars and expansions, shaping Rome's position in Latium.

This next chapter will show us that the Republic, though successful in some ways, faced big internal challenges. The plebeians would not rest until they secured fair treatment and a say in the government that affected their lives.

CHAPTER 5

STRUGGLES OF THE EARLY REPUBLIC

The Seeds of Conflict

At the close of the monarchy and the dawn of the Republic, power in Rome remained in the hands of **patricians**—the old noble families who traced their ancestry to the first senators appointed by Romulus (or so they claimed). Meanwhile, the majority of Roman citizens were **plebeians**, common people who had little direct influence in government.

Even though the Roman Republic had assemblies in which citizens could vote, these assemblies were structured so that the wealthy patricians (and a handful of wealthy plebeians) held most of the power. The rules for voting were based on property classes, meaning that votes of the rich outweighed those of the poor. Many plebeians felt shut out of important decisions. They often struggled with **debt**, **heavy military service**, and **unfair laws** interpreted by patrician judges.

These issues built up until they exploded in what historians call the **Conflict of the Orders**—a long series of political disputes, protests, and reforms. During this period, plebeians fought for and gradually won rights such as the **Tribune of the Plebs**, the **Twelve Tables of Law**, and eventually the right to hold the highest offices. This chapter will examine the early stages of that struggle, showing how Rome's social tensions affected its growth and set the stage for the future.

The First Secession of the Plebs (c. 494 BC)

Debt Crisis

One main reason for plebeian anger was the **debt crisis**. Frequent wars meant that small farmers sometimes could not keep up with loan payments, especially if their fields were ravaged by fighting or they were absent serving in the army. If they defaulted on debts, they could be sold into debt bondage—basically becoming indentured servants to their creditors.

This system seemed unfair because these same plebeians were risking their lives in the army to defend Rome, yet they could lose their land and freedom if they could not pay debts. Patricians, who had more wealth, rarely faced such hardships, and many patricians actually benefited by acquiring lands from bankrupt plebeians.

Walking Out of the City

Tensions boiled over around 494 BC. According to Roman tradition, plebeian soldiers simply walked off the battlefield or refused to serve, then **withdrew to a hill** outside the city (some sources call it the Mons Sacer, or Sacred Mount). This act of protest was later called the **"Secession of the Plebs."**

The patricians panicked. Without the plebeian soldiers, Rome could not defend itself. They sent negotiators to talk with the protesters. Eventually, a compromise was reached: the plebeians returned in exchange for certain concessions, the most important being the creation of new officials to protect plebeian interests.

The Tribune of the Plebs

The chief victory of this secession was the establishment of the **Tribune of the Plebs** (Tribuni Plebis). These tribunes were plebeian officials with the power to:

- **Veto** actions by consuls or other magistrates if those actions harmed the plebeians.
- **Protect** plebeians from unjust treatment. Any attack on a tribune's person was considered a grave crime (the tribune's body was declared "sacrosanct").

At first, there were two tribunes, but over time the number increased. The creation of tribunes was a major step in giving plebeians a voice. Now they had officials whose main job was to speak for them and shield them from exploitation.

Early Roman Law and the Twelve Tables

Lack of Written Laws

Before the Tribune of the Plebs was created, laws were generally unwritten. Patrician judges could interpret custom as they pleased, often unfairly against plebeians. After the tribune office was set up, plebeians demanded that the laws be **written down**. They argued that if laws were public and clear, judges could not twist them.

The Decemviri and the Twelve Tables

Around 451–450 BC, Rome appointed a special commission of ten men, called the **Decemviri**, to write down the laws. These men produced what became known as the **Law of the Twelve Tables**. Although we do not have the complete text today, we know some of its contents from later writers. The Twelve Tables covered:

- **Legal procedures and courts**
- **Debts and property rights**
- **Inheritance and family law**
- **Crimes and punishments**

The laws were harsh by modern standards, but they were an important step. They were displayed publicly (tradition says on bronze tablets) in the Forum so that every citizen could see them. This helped reduce the patricians' ability to manipulate legal rules in secret.

Outcome and Limitations

The Twelve Tables gave plebeians more clarity, but they did not solve everything. Debt laws were still tough, and social inequality remained. Plebeians kept pushing for further reforms, such as the right to hold higher offices and to marry patricians (which was initially forbidden). Still, the Twelve Tables are often called the foundation of Roman law. They stayed in effect long afterward, shaping how later Romans thought about justice.

Other Reforms and Continuing Struggles

The Right to Marry Patricians (Lex Canuleia, 445 BC)

One early restriction was that plebeians could not legally marry patricians. This kept high status strictly among patrician families. In 445 BC, the **Lex Canuleia** changed this, allowing **intermarriage** between the classes. This was a symbolic victory for plebeians, showing that some social barriers were starting to crumble.

Military Tribunes with Consular Power

Around the mid-5th century BC, there was an experiment: instead of electing two consuls (both patricians), sometimes the Romans elected several **military tribunes with consular power**. These tribunes could be plebeians or patricians. It was a compromise aimed at giving plebeians a chance to hold higher office. However, it did not become permanent, and consuls eventually returned as the main executive officials. Still, it showed that plebeians were making progress in winning equal rights.

Continuing Debt Problems

Despite some reforms, **debt** continued to plague plebeians. Whenever wars went badly, farmers were hit hard. Some laws tried to limit debt slavery or reduce interest rates, but it remained a source of recurring conflict. Tribunes often demanded debt relief, while patricians argued that contracts had to be honored. This argument did not go away for centuries.

Outside Pressures: Wars with Neighbors

While these internal struggles raged, Rome kept fighting wars around Latium. Frequent attacks by the **Aequi**, **Volsci**, or nearby Etruscan cities forced Romans to stay militarily strong. Plebeian soldiers who left their fields to fight felt more frustrated when they returned home to find debts piling up. Yet these wars also gave plebeians leverage: the Republic needed them in the army, so tribunes could demand reforms to keep them loyal.

One famous figure from these wars is **Lucius Quinctius Cincinnatus**. He was a patrician farmer chosen as dictator in a crisis against the Aequi around 458 BC. A dictator, in Roman terms, was a temporary official with near-absolute power, appointed for up to six months in emergencies. According to legend, Cincinnatus defeated the enemy quickly, then gave up his power and returned to his farm. Romans saw this as a prime example of **civic virtue**—leading when needed, then stepping down.

Political Tensions and Further Reforms

In Part 1 of this chapter, we learned about the **Secession of the Plebs** around 494 BC, which led to the creation of the **Tribune of the Plebs**. We also discussed the **Twelve Tables** (c. 451–450 BC), the first written Roman laws. These milestones eased some tensions between the patricians (wealthy nobles) and the plebeians (common folk). However, many problems remained. Debts continued to burden plebeian farmers, and patricians still held most of the top offices.

Over the following decades, the plebeians pushed for more changes. At times, this struggle was peaceful, with tribunes proposing new laws or blocking harmful ones. At other times, it led to more **secessions** or threats of revolt. Eventually, a series of political victories allowed plebeians to gain access to almost all official positions and to share in the rewards of Rome's success.

The Role of the Tribunes

The **Tribunes of the Plebs** quickly became powerful voices. Since they could **veto** actions by the consuls or the Senate, the tribunes effectively prevented new laws or decrees that might hurt plebeians. However, some tribunes were more active and brave than others. Occasionally, a tribune might be bribed or persuaded by patricians to stay quiet. But in general, the tribunes were seen as protectors of ordinary citizens.

To support their work, the plebeians also created the **Concilium Plebis** (Council of the Plebs), an assembly of plebeians that could pass **plebiscites**—resolutions applying to plebeians. Over time, these plebiscites could gain the force of law for the entire Roman people, depending on Senate approval and later reforms.

Notable Conflicts and Laws

Lex Canuleia (445 BC)

We already saw how this law allowed marriage between patricians and plebeians. It might seem like a small matter, but it opened the door to family alliances. Now, a wealthy plebeian could marry a patrician woman (or vice versa), creating social ties that could change the city's power structure.

Military Tribunes with Consular Power

For a while, in some years, the people elected **Military Tribunes with Consular Power** instead of the usual two consuls. Sometimes these tribunes were patricians, sometimes plebeians. The exact rules changed over time. This system did not last permanently, but it gave plebeians a chance to occupy a higher office, even if only briefly. Eventually, the tradition of having two consuls each year returned, but the idea that plebeians could hold top positions was growing stronger.

The Second Secession (449 BC)

Tensions flared up again around 449 BC, during the time of the **Decemviri** (the men who wrote the Twelve Tables). The leader of the Decemviri, Appius Claudius, was accused of abusing his power and trying to make himself a tyrant. He also became entangled in a scandal involving a plebeian girl named **Verginia**, whom he tried to claim as a slave. Outraged, the plebeians again **seceded** to the Sacred Mount. This forced the patricians to restore tribune powers and end the Decemviri's rule. Appius Claudius was punished, and the plebeians returned to the city.

Lex Licinia Sextia (367 BC)

One of the biggest breakthroughs came in 367 BC with the **Licinian-Sextian Laws**, proposed by two tribunes, **Lucius Sextius** and **Gaius Licinius Stolo**. These laws addressed the following:

1. **Consulship for Plebeians:** At least one of the two consuls each year could be a plebeian. This opened the highest office in Rome to commoners.
2. **Limiting Public Land Use:** The laws tried to limit how much public land (ager publicus) one person could hold, to reduce patrician abuse of land ownership.

3. **Debt Reforms:** They tried to relieve some burdens by allowing payments of old debts in installments and including interest already paid in the principal.

Though not all details were perfectly enforced, the Lex Licinia Sextia was a major step toward plebeian equality. Soon after, **Lucius Sextius** became the first plebeian consul, showing that real change was possible.

Rome's Continued Wars

The City's Military Obligations

Throughout these internal struggles, Rome stayed busy fighting outside enemies, such as the Volsci, Aequi, Etruscans, and neighboring Latin towns. Plebeians were vital to the army, which gave them a bargaining chip: the city needed their service. If plebeians felt mistreated, they could threaten to refuse military duty or to secede again. This balance of power pushed patricians to compromise at times.

The Gallic Sack of Rome (c. 390 BC)

A dramatic event shook Rome in about 390 BC when a group of **Gauls** (Celtic warriors from beyond the Alps) invaded northern Italy and eventually reached Rome. In a shocking episode, the Gauls defeated the Roman army at the River Allia. They then marched into the city and **sacked** it, burning buildings and causing widespread panic. Many Romans fled to the **Capitoline Hill**, where they held out until they either paid a ransom or found a way to force the Gauls to leave.

This disaster left deep scars on the Roman psyche. It also forced Romans to rebuild their city walls and improve their military. Although the Gauls' stay in Rome was brief, the memory of the **Sack of Rome** would linger, reminding Romans that they had to be constantly prepared for unexpected threats.

Renewed Unity

Oddly enough, the Gallic Sack also brought Romans closer together. Patricians and plebeians realized they had a common interest in defending their homeland. Right after the sack, there were fresh calls for reform. The city had to be rebuilt, farmland restored, and the army reorganized. The fear of another invasion made both classes more willing to work together—for a time.

More Progress for Plebeians

The First Plebeian Dictator

In emergencies, Rome appointed a **dictator** for up to six months. This official had almost total authority to handle the crisis. Over time, plebeians gained the right to be named dictator, too. Having a plebeian dictator signaled trust in plebeian leadership during dire situations.

The Ogulnian Law (300 BC)

This law opened the highest priesthoods (the **Pontifex Maximus** and the college of pontifices) to plebeians. Roman religion was closely tied to government, so letting plebeians become top priests further broke patrician control.

The Hortensian Law (287 BC)

A final key milestone in the Conflict of the Orders was the **Lex Hortensia**, passed in 287 BC. It declared that **plebiscites** (resolutions passed by the Council of the Plebs) were binding on the entire Roman people, including patricians, **without** needing Senate approval. This change made the plebeian assembly an equal lawmaking body, ending most legal differences between patricians and plebeians.

By around 287 BC, the struggle for full legal equality was largely complete, though social and economic inequalities still existed. A new ruling class formed—a **"nobility"**—made up of wealthy patricians and plebeians, united by shared interests. Ordinary plebeians still worked hard to survive, but at least the law no longer excluded them from holding high offices or using the political system to defend their rights.

Everyday Life During the Conflict

Despite the many political disputes, life in Rome went on. Farmers tilled their fields, markets sold goods, and families visited temples to pray to the gods. But the atmosphere could be tense when rumors spread about new laws or debt crises. If a tribune blocked a Senate measure or a consul threatened to crack down on plebeians, crowds might gather in the Forum to protest.

Many plebeians found relief in small victories like land distributions after successful wars or debt reforms that reduced crushing interest rates. Some managed to rise in society by gaining wealth through trade or by serving with distinction in the army. Others remained in poverty, depending on daily labor or the goodwill of patrons.

The Army Evolves

During these struggles, the Roman **army** also underwent changes. The old method of drafting citizen-farmers continued, but repeated warfare meant Rome needed better organization. Soldiers were grouped by wealth and age into "classes," which determined their equipment. The richest could afford helmets, shields, and armor, while the poorest fought with slings or simple spears.

Each **century** (a group of 80–100 men) elected its own leader, called a **centurion**. Though plebeians made up most of the rank and file, the officers tended to be from wealthier backgrounds. Over time, as more plebeians gained wealth and status, some became officers, showing that the army, too, reflected the city's changing social structures.

Religious Life and Festivals

Romans relied heavily on the favor of their gods, especially in these uncertain times. Major gods included Jupiter, Juno, and Minerva, who were worshiped in temples on the Capitoline Hill. Priests performed **sacrifices** before battles, harvests, and important votes. Festivals like the **Lupercalia** (linked to the legend of the she-wolf) continued each year, reminding Romans of their mythical origins.

Religious celebrations were moments of unity when political fights could be set aside—at least for a short while. Everyone, patrician and plebeian alike, wanted the gods on Rome's side.

Art, Architecture, and Culture

During the 5th and 4th centuries BC, Roman art and architecture were still quite simple compared to later centuries. They learned from the **Etruscans** and from Greek colonies in southern Italy.

Temples with columns and triangular pediments were built in the Forum and on the city's hills. Clay figurines and simple pottery were common household items.

Rich families might decorate their homes with small statues or painted vases. However, Rome was still far from the grandeur it would achieve during the late Republic and Empire. The city was known more for its strong soldiers and effective government than for fancy art or literature at this point. Yet seeds of Roman culture were being planted.

Key Figures of the Late Conflict Period

1. **Marcus Furius Camillus (died c. 365 BC):** A patrician general and statesman, sometimes called the "Second Founder of Rome." He led victories against the Veii (an important Etruscan city) and helped rebuild Rome after the Gallic Sack. He also supported some plebeian reforms, acting as a mediator in social disputes.

2. **Gaius Licinius Stolo and Lucius Sextius Lateranus (the Licinian-Sextian Tribunes):** They championed plebeian causes in the mid-4th century BC, passing laws that opened the consulship to plebeians. Lucius Sextius himself became the first plebeian consul.

3. **Quintus Hortensius:** A dictator appointed during more social unrest in 287 BC. He passed the **Lex Hortensia**, ending the need for Senate approval of plebiscites. After that, the Concilium Plebis had full legislative power.

Each of these individuals contributed to Rome's ongoing transformation from a city ruled by a few noble families to a broader-based republic (though still not a modern democracy). Their stories illustrated how the Romans valued both tradition and the willingness to change if it made the city stronger.

Looking Back on the Conflict of the Orders

By the early 3rd century BC, the major points of the Conflict of the Orders were settled:

- Plebeians could marry patricians (Lex Canuleia).
- Plebeians could be consuls (Lex Licinia Sextia).
- Plebeian assembly decisions applied to all Romans (Lex Hortensia).
- Debt and land reforms were attempted, though they were not always fully successful.

An important result was the rise of a **combined aristocracy** often called the "nobility," made up of old patrician families and the wealthiest plebeians. Together, they dominated political life, but the door was no longer closed to plebeians as it had been in the early Republic. Though everyday people still faced hardships, at least the path to power was not completely blocked by one's birth.

Transition to Rome's Wider Ambitions

With internal struggles calmer, Rome turned more attention to expansion across Italy. Having a united citizen body—where both patricians and plebeians could serve as leaders—gave Rome a stronger base for military campaigns. New alliances and wars with neighboring regions would soon reshape the entire peninsula.

In the next chapter, **Chapter 6: Expansion Across Italy**, we will see how Rome's conflicts with the **Samnites**, **Latins**, and other peoples led to Roman control of most of the peninsula. We will also explore how the city built roads, extended citizenship or partial citizenship to conquered peoples, and tested its growing power in new ways. The social reforms of the 5th and 4th centuries BC played a big part in making that expansion possible because they created a more unified Roman state.

CHAPTER 6

EXPANSION ACROSS ITALY

Rome Looks Beyond Latium

By the early 4th century BC, Rome had weathered internal class struggles and major external threats like the Gauls. With the city largely rebuilt and a more inclusive political system in place, Romans turned their ambitions outward. They did not have a grand plan to conquer all of Italy, but circumstances led them into conflicts and alliances that steadily grew their territory.

In this chapter, we will explore how Rome fought the **Samnites**, brought other Latin cities under its control, and managed to extend its influence across the peninsula. We will see how Roman roads, colonies, and citizenship policies helped them keep newly won lands loyal. By the end of this period, Rome was no longer just a leading city in Latium—it was the dominant power in Italy.

The Samnite Wars

One of Rome's biggest challenges came from a people called the **Samnites**. They lived in the mountainous areas of south-central Italy. The Samnites were tough warriors and skilled at fighting in rugged terrain. Rome clashed with them in a series of conflicts known as the **Samnite Wars**.

The First Samnite War (343–341 BC)

Legend says that the First Samnite War began when a city called Capua asked Rome for help against the Samnites. Rome agreed, seeing a chance to gain influence in Campania, a rich farming region near the coast. After a few battles, both sides made peace. This war did not drastically change boundaries, but it signaled that Rome was willing to intervene beyond its immediate neighborhood.

The Latin War (341–338 BC)

Right after the First Samnite War, Rome faced rebellion from some of its old Latin allies. These allies, known as the **Latin League**, felt Rome was becoming too dominant and wanted equal rights or independence. The resulting **Latin War** (341-338 BC) ended in a decisive Roman victory. Rome dissolved the Latin League, bringing the Latin cities under tighter control. Some cities got partial Roman citizenship, while others became allies with specific conditions. This approach—offering different levels of citizenship or alliance—became a Roman trademark, ensuring loyalty.

The Second Samnite War (326–304 BC)

Tensions with the Samnites soon flared up again. The Second Samnite War was much larger and more serious. Rome built a key road called the **Via Appia** (Appian Way) to connect Rome with Capua, making troop movements easier. But the Samnites were fierce opponents, and the Romans suffered a famous defeat at the **Battle of the Caudine Forks** (321 BC). At Caudine Forks, Roman soldiers were trapped in a mountain pass and forced to pass under a "yoke" (a humiliating ritual) after surrendering. This event was a major blow to Roman pride.

Yet Rome did not give up. They reorganized the army, built more roads, and continued to fight. After many campaigns, the Samnites agreed to peace, with Rome gaining territories and influence in southern Italy.

The Third Samnite War (298–290 BC)

Only a few years passed before war broke out again. The Samnites formed a coalition with other foes, including some Gauls who had settled in northern Italy. Despite facing multiple enemies, Rome managed to win a key victory at the **Battle of Sentinum** (295 BC). This victory broke the coalition, and by 290 BC, the Samnites were forced to accept Roman terms.

Though they remained a proud people, the Samnites could not stand against Rome's persistent warfare, better roads, and the loyalty of many allies. Rome emerged as the main power in central and southern Italy. The wars were costly for both sides, but they taught the Romans important lessons about mountain warfare, the need for strong roads, and the value of forging alliances.

Roads, Colonies, and Allies

Rome's success did not come only from its army. The Romans had a clever way of integrating conquered or allied cities. They often:

1. **Built Roads:** After conquering or forming alliances, Rome built roads like the **Via Appia** and the **Via Latina** to move troops and supplies quickly. These roads also helped trade and communication, tying the peninsula together.
2. **Founded Colonies:** The Romans established **colonies** of Roman citizens or Latin allies in strategic locations. These colonies served as military outposts and spread Roman culture. Settlers got farmland in exchange for defending the area.
3. **Granted Different Levels of Citizenship:** Rome did not force a single model on everyone. Some communities got **full Roman citizenship**, others got **Latin Rights** (which had fewer privileges), and others became **allies** (socii) with obligations to supply troops but no direct say in Roman governance. This flexible system made conquered peoples less likely to revolt.

These policies created a network of cities that felt tied to Rome in some way, whether through shared citizenship, partial rights, or alliances. Over time, these connections laid the groundwork for a united Italy under Roman leadership.

Expanding Influence in Northern Italy

The Etruscans and the Gauls

While the Samnite Wars occupied much of Rome's attention in the south, northern Italy also demanded focus. The Etruscan cities still existed, though many had lost power. Meanwhile, Gaulish tribes sometimes raided down through the Po Valley. After the painful memory of the Gallic Sack in 390 BC, Romans built better fortifications and occasionally fought Gaulish tribes.

By the early 3rd century BC, Rome had subdued several Etruscan cities and reached treaties with others, placing them within Rome's alliance system. The Gauls remained a danger, but Rome's expanding network of roads and allies gave it more security than before.

Umbrians, Picenes, and Others

Besides Etruscans and Gauls, the Romans also encountered tribes like the **Umbrians** and **Picenes** in central Italy. Some of these peoples became allies or were incorporated into Roman territory. Step by step, Rome's sphere of influence crept north, though full control over the Po Valley would come later.

Pyrrhus and the Greek Cities of Southern Italy

Tarentum Calls for Help

The Greek colonies in southern Italy (collectively called **Magna Graecia**) watched Rome's expansion with alarm. One city, **Tarentum**, had a naval treaty with Rome, which the Romans allegedly broke by sending ships too close to Tarentum's harbor. Feeling threatened, Tarentum sought help from a Greek king named **Pyrrhus of Epirus**, a skilled general with an army that included war elephants.

The Pyrrhic War (280–275 BC)

Pyrrhus landed in southern Italy in 280 BC. He believed he could unite the Greek cities and drive out the Romans. Initially, he won battles, like the one at **Heraclea**, thanks to his elephants and the shock they caused among Roman troops. But each victory came at a heavy cost in soldiers—hence the term "Pyrrhic victory," meaning a win that is so costly it almost feels like a defeat.

The Romans refused to surrender. They rebuilt their forces, kept allies loyal, and fought Pyrrhus again and again. Pyrrhus moved to Sicily for a while to help Greek cities there against Carthage, but he achieved little. When he returned to Italy, the Romans had adapted to his tactics. He left Italy in 275 BC, effectively giving up.

This war showed that Rome could stand up to a top Greek general and large war elephants. It also led many Greek cities in southern Italy to accept Roman leadership. By 272 BC, Tarentum itself fell under Roman control. Rome now had a major foothold in the south.

The Unification of Italy Under Rome

By around 265 BC, Rome was the dominant power from the Arno River in the north down to the tip of the peninsula in the south. Various peoples—Etruscans, Latins, Samnites, Greeks, and others—were tied to Rome by treaties, colonies, or citizenship arrangements. This did not mean everyone was happy, but the system largely worked. The Romans allowed local customs and some self-rule, so long as communities supplied troops when needed and did not rebel.

As a result, Rome could draw on a large pool of manpower for its armies. Soldiers came from all over Italy to fight under Roman command. This manpower advantage would be crucial in the next great test: **the Punic Wars** against Carthage. But before we jump ahead, let us explore more about how life changed within Italy due to Roman expansion.

Impact of Expansion on Roman Society

With new territories came new wealth, resources, and responsibilities. Romans gained access to rich farmland in Campania and Apulia, as well as trade routes along the coast. War spoils funded building projects. But expansion also created new tensions:

1. **Land Distribution:** Many patricians and wealthy plebeians took a large share of conquered land. Ordinary soldiers sometimes received smaller plots or had to wait for official colonies to be founded.
2. **Cultural Mixing:** Roman culture spread, but the Romans also picked up ideas from the Greeks, Etruscans, and others. This influenced art, religion, and daily life.

3. **Military Obligations:** Allied cities had to send troops, but they did not have the same privileges as full Roman citizens. Over time, this difference would spark new demands for rights, though not until much later.

Nevertheless, at this stage, most allies stayed loyal because Roman rule, while sometimes strict, also offered protection from other enemies and a share in Rome's successes.

Strengthening Infrastructure

Roads and Communication

One of the biggest factors in Rome's success was its **road system**. By the early 3rd century BC, key roads included:

- **Via Appia** (from Rome to Capua, eventually extended to Brundisium on the Adriatic Sea).
- **Via Latina** (toward the south and east).
- **Via Salaria** (the ancient salt route heading northeast).

These roads were well-built, with layers of stone and gravel, allowing armies and merchants to move in all weather. Travel times were faster than in many other ancient states, helping Rome respond quickly to uprisings or invasions.

Aqueducts and Urban Improvements

As Rome's power grew, so did its city. Early aqueducts like the **Aqua Appia** (built in 312 BC) brought fresh water from nearby hills into the city. Public buildings, temples, and forums were renovated or expanded. The city's population rose, and more people moved in from allied regions. Though still not as splendid as it would be in later centuries, Rome was becoming a bustling center.

Everyday Life in a Growing Republic

Trade and Markets

With more territory under Roman control, trade expanded. Merchants could travel safely along roads and by sea (in the Tyrrhenian and Adriatic waters). Goods like grain, olives, wine, livestock, and metals moved in and out of Rome. New markets opened in the Forum, and wealthy families profited by investing in trade ventures.

Social Classes and Politics

The old conflict between patricians and plebeians cooled, replaced by a new **elite** or **nobility** formed from both groups. Families who rose to the consulship or other high offices were considered part of the ruling class. However, many common people still lived in modest conditions. Some found opportunities in the army or by migrating to colonies for fresh farmland.

Political competition continued among leading families, who vied for consulships and other magistracies. But for the moment, unity was stronger than division because foreign wars demanded cooperation.

Citizenship and Identity

As Rome spread, questions arose: Who was a Roman citizen? Who was merely an ally? The Romans had several categories:

- **Full Roman Citizens:** Mostly in the city of Rome, its colonies, and some incorporated communities. Full citizens could vote in Roman assemblies and hold office (if male).
- **Citizens Without Voting Rights:** Some communities were granted Roman citizenship but did not have the right to vote. This status usually improved over time.

- **Latin Rights:** People in Latin colonies had a certain legal status between full Roman citizenship and ally status. They could do business and marry Romans under Roman law.
- **Allies (Socii):** These communities had treaties with Rome. They were expected to provide troops but kept some local autonomy. They usually could not vote in Rome.

This flexible system made conquered or allied peoples feel they could eventually gain more privileges if they stayed loyal. It was a clever way to integrate diverse groups.

Key Battles and Events of the Period

1. **Battle of Caudine Forks (321 BC):** Rome's humiliating defeat in the Second Samnite War.
2. **Battle of Sentinum (295 BC):** A major Roman victory that ended the serious threat of Samnite-Gallic-Etruscan alliance.
3. **Pyrrhic War (280–275 BC):** King Pyrrhus's arrival with elephants, his early wins, and ultimate failure against Rome.
4. **Fall of Tarentum (272 BC):** Rome takes over the Greek city after Pyrrhus leaves Italy.

These battles tested Rome's resilience. Each time, the city recovered from defeat or overcame tough opponents, building confidence and a reputation for persistence.

Roman Colonies and Their Role

Rome founded many **colonies** in conquered regions. These colonies were not just for controlling territory; they also helped relieve population pressure in Rome by giving land to poor citizens. Colonies became mini-versions of Rome, with similar laws, a forum, and walls. Colonists were often veterans who could defend the area.

Examples of early colonies include places like:

- **Ostia** (though very close to Rome, important for salt and trade).
- **Cales** in Campania.
- **Luceria** in Apulia.

Colonies turned conquered lands into loyal outposts, spreading Roman culture and ensuring a steady supply of soldiers in case of new wars.

Early Relations with Carthage

Although we will cover the **Punic Wars** in a later chapter, it is worth noting that during this period, Rome had not yet clashed seriously with **Carthage**, a powerful city in North Africa. They had some treaties and even cooperated occasionally (for example, Carthage once offered help against King Pyrrhus in Sicily). But tensions existed because both Rome and Carthage wanted to control trade routes, especially around Sicily.

This rivalry would eventually explode into open war, but for now, Rome was primarily focused on Italy. Carthage still saw Rome as a rising power but had not fully realized how big a threat it would become. The seeds of conflict were being planted as both sides watched each other's moves.

Social and Cultural Shifts During Expansion

Greek Influence

With Rome taking over Greek cities in the south, Greek culture began to influence Roman life. Wealthy Romans admired Greek art, hired Greek tutors to teach their children, and learned the Greek language. Greek gods sometimes merged with Roman gods, and Greek myths found their way into Roman literature. This cultural blending would grow stronger over time, shaping everything from Roman philosophy to architecture.

Changes in Warfare

Facing foes like the Samnites in the mountains forced the Roman army to adapt. They developed more flexible formations, learned how to fight in rough terrain, and built fortifications faster. Through contact with Greek cities, they also learned about fighting styles used by Greek hoplites and war elephants (from Pyrrhus). All this experience turned Rome into a more versatile military power.

Growth of Slave Labor

Each war brought more prisoners, some of whom were sold as slaves. Rich landowners used these slaves on large farms (called **latifundia**), especially in fertile regions like Campania. While this practice did not yet dominate Roman agriculture, it was increasing. Over time, the rise of slave labor would create tensions, as it undercut the small farmer's ability to compete. But those problems would become more severe in the late Republic.

Notable Leaders of the Era

1. **Appius Claudius Caecus (4th–3rd century BC):** A leading statesman who built the **Via Appia** and the **Aqua Appia** (Rome's first aqueduct). He was a strong-willed censor and consul who championed public works.
2. **Publius Decius Mus (two figures, father and son):** Consuls famous for a ritual of **devotio**, sacrificing their own lives in battle to bring victory to Rome. The father did so at the Battle of Vesuvius (340 BC) against the Latins, and the son at Sentinum (295 BC) against the Samnites and Gauls.

3. **Fabricius Luscinus:** A Roman commander admired by Pyrrhus for his honesty. Legend says Pyrrhus tried to bribe Fabricius with gold, but Fabricius refused. This story showed Roman virtue, at least in the eyes of later writers.

Toward a Dominant Presence in Italy

By about 270 BC, Rome controlled most of the peninsula. The big difference from earlier powers like the Etruscans was that Rome knew how to build lasting ties with the cities it defeated. Instead of crushing them completely, Rome integrated them into its system of roads, colonies, and alliances. This approach gave Rome access to far greater manpower than any single city-state could muster.

When a new war came along, many Italians fought side by side with Roman legions. They might not have had full Roman citizenship, but they were bound to the city by treaties and the possibility of gaining more rights in the future. This method, combined with Rome's determined spirit, made the Republic a force that no single Italian people could overcome.

CHAPTER 7

THE WARS WITH CARTHAGE

Setting the Stage

By the middle of the 3rd century BC, Rome controlled most of the Italian Peninsula. Through alliances, colonies, and determined warfare, the city had become the strongest power in Italy. Yet Rome was not the only major force in the western Mediterranean. Across the sea, on the North African coast, lay the wealthy city-state of **Carthage**. Founded by Phoenicians centuries earlier, Carthage was rich in trade, had a powerful navy, and held territories in places like Sardinia, Corsica, and parts of Sicily.

Carthage and Rome had cooperated from time to time, even signing treaties. But both were growing powers with overlapping interests—especially in Sicily, a large island south of Italy. Soon, their competition turned into open conflict. The battles that followed are known as the **Punic Wars** (from "Punicus," the Latin word for Phoenician/Carthaginian). These wars lasted over a century and shaped the destiny of Rome, making it a major naval and imperial power.

In this first part of Chapter 7, we will explore the causes of the First Punic War, how the Romans built a navy from almost nothing, and how they ultimately claimed victory over Carthage on the seas and in Sicily. We will see that Rome's dogged determination, combined with its expanding manpower, allowed it to challenge and defeat a maritime giant.

Rome and Carthage: Two Rising Powers

Carthage's Background

Carthage began as a colony of the ancient Phoenicians from the city of Tyre (in the eastern Mediterranean). Over centuries, it grew into a powerful commercial hub. Carthaginian traders sailed far and wide, exchanging goods like metals, textiles, and food. Carthage's strength rested largely on its **navy**—it had skilled sailors and a tradition of building strong warships, especially **quinqueremes** (large galleys with multiple rows of oars).

Carthage also governed territories outside Africa, especially on the islands of **Sicily**, **Sardinia**, and **Corsica**, plus parts of southern Spain. It often hired mercenary soldiers (warriors from different lands who fought for pay). The Carthaginians were wealthy, but much of their military might depended on these hired troops and on local allies rather than on a large pool of citizen-soldiers.

Rome's Ambitions

Rome, on the other hand, had a citizen-army tradition. Most of its fighters were Roman or Italian allies who served out of a sense of duty, loyalty, or the hope of spoils. By 264 BC, Rome had never fought a major power beyond Italy. Carthage, with its vast trade network, outmatched Rome in naval skills. But Rome believed it could adapt.

The main flashpoint was **Sicily**, a rich island close to Italy. It was partly under Carthaginian influence, partly inhabited by Greek city-states, and partly within Rome's sphere of interest. When a group of Italian mercenaries called the **Mamertines** seized the city of Messana in northeastern Sicily, both Rome and Carthage got drawn in. This local crisis lit the fuse of the First Punic War.

The First Punic War (264–241 BC)

The War Begins

In 264 BC, Rome decided to help the Mamertines in Messana, while Carthage took the opposing side. The Romans likely saw a chance to extend their control into Sicily. At first, Carthage dominated at sea. Their navy blockaded ports and cut off Roman supplies. On land, Roman legions could hold their own, but they needed to find a way to challenge Carthage on the water.

Building a Roman Navy

Rome was not famous for sailing. Yet the Senate realized they had to create a fleet if they wanted to match Carthage's might. They began constructing warships, supposedly using a captured Carthaginian quinquereme as a model. Roman shipbuilders learned fast, though they made simpler versions at first.

To make up for inexperience at sea, the Romans invented a device called the **corvus** (Latin for "crow"). It was a hinged boarding bridge with a sharp spike at the end. When a Roman ship got close to an enemy vessel, the corvus would drop and attach, turning the naval battle into something like a land battle, where Roman infantry could storm across and fight hand-to-hand. This innovation helped offset Carthage's advantage in naval maneuvers, though it made Roman ships heavier and harder to steer.

Key Battles at Sea

- **Battle of Mylae (260 BC):** One of Rome's earliest naval victories. Using the corvus, the Roman fleet under Gaius Duilius defeated Carthaginian ships. After the battle, Duilius erected a column in Rome to celebrate.

- **Battle of Ecnomus (256 BC):** A huge clash, sometimes considered one of the largest naval battles of the ancient world. Romans again won, letting them land an army in North Africa, hoping to bring the war close to Carthage.

These victories shocked the Carthaginians. They had never seen Rome perform so well at sea. The Romans proved that their determination and willingness to learn could overcome decades of Carthaginian naval tradition.

Roman Invasion of Africa

Around 256 BC, the Romans attempted to invade North Africa to force Carthage to surrender. They had some initial successes under **Marcus Atilius Regulus**, who marched near Carthage's outskirts. However, the Carthaginians hired a Spartan general named Xanthippus, who reorganized their forces and used war elephants effectively. In a major engagement, Regulus was defeated and captured. This setback taught Rome that Carthage could still defend its home turf well.

Stalemate and Final Victory

For several more years, both sides battled in Sicily and at sea. Each side won some encounters, lost others. Storms also wrecked Roman fleets more than once, causing heavy losses of men and ships. War exhaustion set in as the fight dragged on.

Finally, the Romans built another fleet in 242 BC and won a decisive sea victory off the Aegates Islands in 241 BC. Carthage, low on funds and manpower, asked for peace. Under the treaty, Carthage gave up all claims to Sicily and paid a large indemnity (sum of money) to Rome. Thus ended the First Punic War. Rome took control of Sicily, making it the first Roman **province** outside Italy—a region governed by a Roman official rather than a local ally arrangement.

Consequences of the First Punic War

- **Rise of Rome's Navy:** Rome proved it could fight at sea, opening doors to wider conquests.
- **Carthage's Financial Strain:** The heavy indemnity and loss of Sicily weakened Carthage's finances.
- **Expansion Outside Italy:** By taking Sicily, Rome officially stepped beyond the Italian Peninsula. Soon after, Rome also took control of Sardinia and Corsica in a somewhat opportunistic move, further shrinking Carthaginian influence.

Still, Carthage was not finished. Many Carthaginians, including the soldier-leader **Hamilcar Barca**, believed they should rebuild power and seek revenge. This desire for revenge eventually led to the Second Punic War, which we will examine in Part 2 of this chapter.

Between the First and Second Punic Wars

After 241 BC, Carthage faced a dangerous rebellion among its own mercenary troops who felt unpaid. Hamilcar Barca suppressed this uprising with brutal determination. He then turned Carthage's eyes toward **Iberia** (Spain) as a place to gain new wealth, silver mines, and soldiers. Meanwhile, Rome solidified control over Sicily, Sardinia, and Corsica.

Rome and Carthage signed a new treaty setting boundaries in Spain, with the **Ebro River** as a limit for Carthaginian expansion. However, the city of **Saguntum** lay south of the Ebro yet claimed friendship with Rome, creating a potential flashpoint. Over the next 20 years, tensions rose again. When Hamilcar's son, **Hannibal**, came to power, the stage was set for one of the most dramatic wars in ancient history.

The Second Punic War (218–201 BC)

Hannibal's Bold Move

Hannibal Barca grew up hating Rome, influenced by his father Hamilcar's bitterness after the First Punic War. In 218 BC, Hannibal attacked Saguntum (an ally of Rome) in Spain, sparking the Second Punic War. Rome demanded he withdraw. Hannibal refused. Instead, he devised a stunning plan: to invade Italy itself by crossing the **Alps** with a large army and war elephants.

This journey was incredibly risky. The cold weather, high altitudes, and hostile tribes in the mountains took a heavy toll on his forces. But Hannibal's determination paid off: he arrived in northern Italy with a smaller but still formidable army, catching the Romans by surprise.

Early Carthaginian Triumphs

- **Battle of the Trebia (218 BC):** Hannibal lured the Roman army across a river in freezing conditions and ambushed them. The Romans lost badly.
- **Battle of Lake Trasimene (217 BC):** Using fog and the narrow terrain near the lake, Hannibal trapped a Roman force under Gaius Flaminius. Thousands of Romans died, and Flaminius himself was slain.
- **Battle of Cannae (216 BC):** Often called Hannibal's masterpiece, Cannae saw Carthaginian forces encircle a much larger Roman army. The Romans suffered a devastating defeat—tens of thousands were killed or captured. Cannae remains a legendary example of battlefield strategy, and it shook Rome to the core.

After these colossal victories, some Italian allies deserted Rome, hoping Hannibal would liberate them. But Hannibal never received strong enough reinforcements from Carthage to fully conquer Rome. Instead, he roamed Italy, hoping more allies would rise against the Romans. Though he caused great destruction, he could not force the city to surrender.

The Roman Response: Fabian Tactics

Following the disaster at Lake Trasimene, the Roman Senate appointed **Quintus Fabius Maximus** as dictator. Fabius decided to avoid large battles with Hannibal, choosing instead to **shadow** his army, block his supply lines, and wear him down. This cautious approach was unpopular at first—many Romans wanted a swift victory. But after the defeat at Cannae, people saw the wisdom in Fabius's tactics. Over time, Hannibal's forces grew weaker as the Romans refused to meet him in open battle.

Publius Cornelius Scipio in Spain

While Hannibal threatened Italy, Rome sent a young general named **Publius Cornelius Scipio** (later called "Scipio Africanus") to fight Carthaginian forces in Spain. Over several years, Scipio defeated Hannibal's brother Hasdrubal and took control of key Carthaginian cities, such as New Carthage (modern Cartagena). By cutting off Carthage's Spanish silver mines and soldier recruits, Scipio reduced Hannibal's lifeline.

The End of the War: Battle of Zama (202 BC)

In 204 BC, Scipio landed in North Africa, forcing the Carthaginians to recall Hannibal from Italy. The two armies finally met at the **Battle of Zama** in 202 BC. Scipio had studied Hannibal's tactics and had cavalry support from Numidian allies. Hannibal's elephants failed to break the Roman lines. In the end, Rome won a decisive victory. Carthage agreed to peace in 201 BC, surrendering its fleet, paying a huge indemnity, and accepting restrictions on future wars.

The Second Punic War was over. Rome emerged stronger, having beaten one of history's greatest generals. Carthage was left politically and financially crippled, though it continued to exist as a trading city under strict Roman watch.

The Third Punic War (149-146 BC)

Rising Hostility in Rome

In the decades after the Second Punic War, Carthage recovered somewhat by focusing on trade. Some Roman politicians, like **Cato the Elder**, became worried that Carthage might regain military strength. Cato famously ended his speeches with "Carthage must be destroyed." Meanwhile, Carthage's neighbor, King Masinissa of Numidia, chipped away at Carthaginian territory, knowing Carthage could not legally go to war without Roman permission.

War Breaks Out

By 149 BC, Carthage finally fought back against Numidia's raids. Rome declared that Carthage had violated the peace treaty. Demanding Carthage's full disarmament and relocation away from the coast, the Romans forced the issue. Carthage refused to abandon its city. War began—this time, the outcome was grim for Carthage.

Siege and Destruction

Rome sent an army to besiege Carthage itself. The Carthaginians bravely resisted for three years, even making new weapons in secret. But by 146 BC, Roman legions under **Scipio Aemilianus** (the grandson by adoption of Scipio Africanus) broke through the walls. The city was captured, burned, and largely destroyed. Surviving inhabitants were sold into slavery. Carthage's lands became the Roman province of **Africa**.

The Third Punic War ended Carthage as a political power forever. Rome now stood unchallenged in the western Mediterranean.

Aftermath of the Punic Wars

By 146 BC, Rome was supreme in the west. Sicily, Sardinia, Corsica, parts of Spain, and North Africa were all under Roman control. The wars had huge impacts on Roman society:

1. **Provincial System:** Rome organized conquered lands into **provinces** governed by Roman officials. Wealth from these provinces flowed into Rome, including grain, taxes, and war spoils.
2. **Rise of the Military Class:** Successful generals gained fame and fortune, paving the way for more ambitious military leaders in the future.
3. **Change in Farming:** An increase in slave labor, combined with cheap grain imports, hurt small farmers in Italy. Over time, this shift would cause social and economic strain.
4. **Naval Dominance:** Rome's navy became the strongest in the western Mediterranean, allowing safer trade routes and easier movement of troops.

Though there were other conflicts going on—such as wars in Spain and with Greek kingdoms—none matched the scale of the struggle against Carthage. The Punic Wars showed Rome's capacity for adaptation, persistence, and resourcefulness. They also revealed that Roman ambition had no clear limit.

CHAPTER 8

TURNING INTO A MEDITERRANEAN POWER

From West to East

Having defeated Carthage, Rome now ruled much of the western Mediterranean. However, the Roman Republic did not stop there. The eastern Mediterranean was full of rich territories dominated by **Greek kingdoms**—descendants of Alexander the Great's empire. Over time, Rome found itself drawn into conflicts and alliances with these states.

In this chapter, we will explore the **Macedonian Wars**, Rome's interventions in Greece and Asia Minor, and how, by the mid-2nd century BC, the Republic controlled nearly the entire Mediterranean coastline. This expansion made Rome both wealthy and powerful, but it also led to new challenges. Ruling a vast empire required new administrative methods, new armies, and new attitudes at home.

Rome Encounters the Hellenistic World

The Hellenistic Kingdoms

After Alexander the Great died in 323 BC, his generals divided his empire into several large kingdoms, including:

- **Macedonia** in northern Greece.
- The **Seleucid** kingdom in Asia (stretching from modern Turkey into parts of the Middle East).
- The **Ptolemaic** kingdom in Egypt.

These "Hellenistic" kingdoms were Greek in culture but ruled over many local peoples. They had professional armies, big cities, and splendid art. Some Greek city-states remained independent or semi-independent, often forming leagues or alliances.

Rome's First Involvements

During the Second Punic War, **Philip V** of Macedonia allied with Hannibal briefly. This caused Rome to keep an eye on the east. After defeating Carthage, Rome punished Philip in the **First Macedonian War** (215–205 BC), though the conflict ended without a decisive Roman victory.

Soon, tensions rose again. Greek city-states like Pergamum and Rhodes asked Rome for help against Macedonia or the Seleucids. Rome, seeing a chance to increase its influence, intervened. Step by step, the Republic got pulled deeper into Greek affairs.

The Second Macedonian War (200–196 BC)

Causes of Conflict

Philip V, still king of Macedonia, threatened the independence of Greek cities. He also clashed with Rhodes and Pergamum, two important allies of Rome. The Roman Senate, wary of Philip's growing power, declared war in 200 BC. Although some Romans hesitated—fighting across the sea seemed risky—others believed it was necessary to protect Roman allies.

Key Battles and Diplomacy

The Romans sent armies to Greece under generals like Titus Quinctius **Flamininus**. They also worked with local Greek allies who feared Macedonia. In 197 BC, Flamininus defeated Philip at the **Battle of Cynoscephalae**, a major confrontation that showed how the Roman legion could outmaneuver the Macedonian phalanx.

With Philip beaten, Rome forced him to surrender much of his fleet, pay an indemnity, and withdraw from Greece. In 196 BC, Flamininus proclaimed the "freedom of the Greeks" at the Isthmian Games, winning local goodwill. Many Greek cities welcomed Rome as a liberator, though some were uneasy about the new power from the west.

Aftermath

Macedonia was weakened but not destroyed. Rome did not yet annex Macedonia as a province, preferring to keep it as a smaller kingdom that would not threaten Greek city-states. Meanwhile, Romans tasted further success, discovering the cultural riches of Greece—fine art, literature, and philosophy that amazed them.

War with the Seleucids and Antiochus III (192–188 BC)

Antiochus III's Ambitions

While Rome dealt with Philip, **Antiochus III** of the Seleucid Empire expanded into Asia Minor and even crossed into Greece. He allied with the famed Carthaginian general **Hannibal**, who had fled to the east after losing the Second Punic War. Worried that Antiochus might replace Philip as a threat, Rome demanded that Antiochus stay out of Greece.

Battles in Greece and Asia Minor

The conflict began in 192 BC when Antiochus marched into Greece, hoping to rally Greek cities against Rome. Instead, he found limited support, and the Romans pushed him back, defeating him at **Thermopylae** (191 BC). Later, a Roman fleet and army crossed to Asia Minor. In 190 BC, at the **Battle of Magnesia**, Roman and allied forces crushed Antiochus's army.

In the peace treaty of Apamea (188 BC), the Seleucids lost most of their territory in Asia Minor. Roman allies like Pergamum gained land, while Rome took no direct province yet—still preferring to govern indirectly. But Rome's footprint in the east grew, and more Greek city-states came under Rome's "protection."

Hannibal's Fate

Hannibal, who advised Antiochus, was not given full command. After the defeat at Magnesia, he fled again. Eventually, cornered by Roman demands for his surrender, Hannibal is said to have taken poison around 183 BC, ending the life of one of history's greatest generals. He never got the second chance to challenge Rome that he had hoped for.

Continued Conflicts in Greece and Macedonia

The Third Macedonian War (171–168 BC)

Philip V was succeeded by his son **Perseus**, who tried to restore Macedonian power. He built alliances and armies, worrying the Greek allies of Rome. As tensions rose, Rome declared war again in 171 BC. After some back-and-forth fighting, the Roman consul **Lucius Aemilius Paullus** defeated Perseus at the **Battle of Pydna** in 168 BC. This battle showed the legion's superiority once more over the phalanx.

Rome broke up Macedonia into smaller regions, placed under Roman oversight, and took hostages from noble families (including young men who might be potential rivals). Greek states that supported Perseus were punished. Although Rome still did not formally annex Macedonia, its control over the region tightened.

The Destruction of Corinth (146 BC)

Only a few years later—coincidentally the same year as Carthage's destruction—Rome faced a revolt by the **Achaean League**, a group of

Greek cities. The Roman army crushed the rebellion and destroyed the city of **Corinth** as a warning. Many of its treasures were taken to Rome. This harsh act signaled the end of widespread Greek independence. From then on, Greece was firmly under Roman influence, soon becoming the province of Achaea.

Rome Moves into Asia Minor

After defeating Antiochus III, Rome allowed friendly kingdoms like **Pergamum** to govern much of Asia Minor. But eventually, conflicts arose with local rulers, such as **King Mithridates** of Pontus (in the 1st century BC). Though this is slightly later than our current focus, it is important to note that Rome's involvement in Asia Minor grew slowly, often through treaties and "requests" from local allies who needed help against stronger neighbors.

By the mid-2nd century BC, Rome was the main power broker in the region. Even if it did not turn every place into a province right away, it dictated terms through alliances or direct interventions.

Administration of Rome's Widening Empire

With territories in Spain, Africa, Greece, and beyond, the Romans faced new governing challenges:

1. **Provinces:** They sent governors (often ex-consuls or ex-praetors) to oversee provinces like Sicily, Nearer Spain (Hispania Citerior), and Farther Spain (Hispania Ulterior). These governors had broad powers to collect taxes and keep order.
2. **Financial Exploitation:** Wealthy Romans sometimes exploited these provinces for personal gain, demanding bribes or stealing local resources. This behavior later caused resentment and revolts.
3. **Military Requirements:** Rome had to keep legions stationed in faraway lands, leading to longer campaigns and the possibility of generals gaining personal loyalty from troops.
4. **Cultural Exchange:** Conquered or allied lands brought new arts, religions, and ideas back to Rome. Greek culture, in particular, fascinated many Romans, who began adopting Greek language, tutors, and luxuries.

These changes affected the social structure of the Republic. A new class of Roman "businessmen" called **publicani** emerged, handling tax collection and large-scale trade in the provinces. Senators grew richer from war spoils, farmland in Italy, and tributes from abroad. Some Romans worried that greed and luxury would corrupt their old virtues of simplicity and discipline.

Social Effects of Rapid Expansion

Growth of Latifundia and Rural Decline

As Rome gained more provinces, cheap grain from places like Sicily and Africa flooded the Italian market. Wealthy landowners bought up small farms, turning them into large estates called **latifundia**. They used **slave labor**—captured in wars—to work these estates at low cost. Meanwhile, many small farmers, especially those who served in the legions for long campaigns, found themselves unable to compete. Some lost their lands or sold them and moved to the city in search of work.

Rise of the Urban Poor

In Rome itself, the population grew. Freedmen, small farmers without land, and others poured into the city. This created an expanding class of **urban poor**, living in crowded apartments or insulae. Wealthy nobles sometimes tried to gain favor with this group by offering food or entertainment. Over time, these crowds became a political force. Ambitious leaders could rally them for votes or demonstrations.

Luxury and Greek Influence

Military victories in the East exposed Romans to Greek art, literature, and styles of living. Wealthy families decorated their homes with Greek statues, mosaics, and expensive furniture. Some Romans admired Greek philosophy, inviting Greek teachers to educate their children. Latin, the Roman language, borrowed words from Greek. This mingling of cultures enriched Roman life but also raised worries that old Roman values—like frugality and strict discipline—might be lost.

New Ideals and Tensions

Some Romans, like Cato the Elder, warned against adopting "foreign" habits. Others embraced Greek learning wholeheartedly. This divide hinted at future cultural struggles. Could Rome remain "Roman" while ruling far-off lands and absorbing so many influences? Nobody had an easy answer, but the city kept changing as its empire grew.

Political Challenges and the Rise of Powerful Generals

Longer Commands

Originally, Roman magistrates (consuls, praetors) served for one year. But with wars taking place far from Italy, the Senate sometimes extended a commander's term. Such an official might become **proconsul** or **propraetor**, keeping imperium (the power to command) for extra years abroad. This shift allowed generals to build closer relationships with their troops, who might come to see them as personal patrons.

Triumphs and Personal Glory

Successful generals returned to Rome to celebrate a **triumph**, a grand parade through the city where the commander displayed captured treasures and prisoners. The people cheered, and the general earned immense prestige. Over time, some generals used their fame to influence politics. Senators, too, craved triumphs to boost their family names.

As Rome's empire stretched across the Mediterranean, the wealth and power of these generals soared. While the Republic's constitution tried to prevent any one man from becoming too powerful, the system struggled to manage large-scale wars and extended commands. A new kind of leadership, based on personal loyalty, began to emerge.

The Final Defeat of Macedonia and Greece as a Province

We saw how Rome fought several Macedonian Wars. After the final rebellion in 149–148 BC, Macedonia became a formal Roman province. In 146 BC, Corinth was destroyed, and soon Greece was placed under tighter Roman authority. Over the next few decades,

Greek city-states lost most of their independence, though they kept many local traditions. Roman officials collected taxes, while Roman merchants set up businesses.

For Romans, Greece became not only a conquered land but also a source of cultural influence. Wealthy young men traveled there to study philosophy or rhetoric in Athens. Artists and intellectuals found patronage in Rome. This blending of Greek and Roman ways is called **Greco-Roman culture**, which would continue developing for centuries.

The Fate of Other Eastern Kingdoms

Pergamum Becomes Roman Territory

In 133 BC, King Attalus III of Pergamum died without heirs. He willed his kingdom to Rome, hoping to avoid a messy succession. This gave Rome direct control of a big part of Asia Minor. The region was organized into the province of **Asia** (not the entire continent, but a portion of western Asia Minor). Rome gained more tax revenue and trade from this area.

The Seleucids and Ptolemies

The Seleucid Empire weakened over time due to internal rebellions and pressure from Parthia in the east. Rome did not fully annex the Seleucid lands at this stage, but it kept them under watch. The Ptolemaic kingdom in Egypt remained independent for now, though it formed close ties with Rome to secure protection. Eventually, these areas would also come under Roman control, but that would happen in future decades and involve famous figures like Cleopatra and Julius Caesar, beyond our current scope.

The Mediterranean as a "Roman Lake"

By the mid-2nd century BC, Rome's reach extended across the entire **mare internum** ("internal sea," what we call the Mediterranean). The Republic directly governed some regions, while others remained client kingdoms or allies. Rome's fleets patrolled the waters to keep pirates in check. Trade increased, bringing grain, metals, wine, and other goods to Italy.

Romans began to speak of the **mare nostrum** ("our sea"). Though not yet complete, the idea of the Mediterranean as a Roman domain was taking shape. This transformation from a regional Italian power to a Mediterranean empire was dramatic and fast, raising questions about how the Republic could handle such vast responsibilities.

CHAPTER 9

SOCIAL CHANGES AND REFORMERS

Rome's Changing Society

By the mid-2nd century BC, Rome had grown from a city-state controlling Italy to a sprawling power with provinces across the Mediterranean. This rapid expansion brought new wealth to Rome—treasures, farmland, and slaves. But it also caused problems. Many small farmers lost their land to large estates, or *latifundia*, operated by wealthy Romans using slave labor. The gap between rich and poor widened. In the city, a growing population of jobless citizens struggled to make ends meet.

These social and economic strains led some Romans to call for reforms. They saw how the old ways that once supported a small republic might not work for a giant empire. They wanted fairer land distribution, better legal rights for the poor, and a check on the power of the elite. This chapter looks at the **Gracchi brothers** and other figures who tried to fix Rome's problems, and how their efforts triggered conflict that sometimes turned violent. Through these struggles, we see cracks in the republican system that would later pave the way for strong military leaders to dominate Rome's politics.

The Decline of the Small Farmer
Conquests and Cheap Grain

When Rome defeated Carthage and took over provinces like Sicily and Africa, it gained vast amounts of farmland. Much of the grain from these new territories was shipped to Rome, sold at low prices or provided as tax payments in kind. This cheap grain undercut small

Italian farmers, who found it hard to compete. Wealthy Romans took advantage of the situation by buying up farmland from struggling families.

The Rise of Latifundia

Wealthy landowners created large estates called **latifundia**, often staffed by slaves captured in foreign wars. These estates produced crops—grain, olives, grapes—on a huge scale. Because slave labor was cheaper than hiring workers, the owners of latifundia could make big profits. Meanwhile, many former small farmers either became tenant farmers on the land they once owned or moved to the city in search of work.

The Urban Poor

In Rome itself, the population swelled with displaced farmers, freed slaves, and others seeking a better life. Many lived in crowded apartment buildings (*insulae*) without steady jobs. Some found day labor, but others depended on handouts or small payments from political patrons. This group, often called the **urban poor**, became a force in politics, since they had the right to vote in the assemblies. Ambitious politicians began trying to win their favor by promising food distributions or other benefits.

Calls for Reform

Some leaders recognized these problems and wanted to help. They believed that a healthy republic needed a strong class of small landowners who could serve in the army and maintain traditional Roman values. But powerful senators and landowners resisted efforts to limit their estates or to redistribute land. This clash would erupt when two young men from a famous family stepped forward—the **Gracchus brothers**.

Tiberius Gracchus

Background

Tiberius Sempronius Gracchus was born around 163–162 BC into a well-known patrician family. His maternal grandfather was **Scipio Africanus**, the hero who defeated Hannibal. Tiberius served in the army and saw firsthand the plight of small soldiers who returned from campaigns to find their farms ruined. Elected as **Tribune of the Plebs** in 133 BC, he used his office to propose bold reforms.

Agrarian Reform Bill

Tiberius noticed that much "public land" (*ager publicus*), gained from conquests, was being used illegally by wealthy families for huge estates. His **agrarian reform bill** aimed to enforce an existing law that limited how much public land one person could hold (often around 500 iugera). Excess land would be taken back by the state and redistributed to poor citizens in small plots. This plan was supposed to revive the class of small farmers and give them a chance to earn a living on their own land.

Opposition and Conflict

Many senators and wealthy landowners fiercely opposed Tiberius's bill. They feared losing their valuable estates. When Tiberius tried to push the law through the Plebeian Assembly, a fellow tribune vetoed him. Tiberius responded by having that tribune removed from office—a controversial move.

Eventually, the assembly passed Tiberius's reform, creating a three-man commission (including Tiberius himself) to oversee land distribution. This alarmed the Senate even more. Rumors spread that Tiberius wanted to stay in office or become king. When Tiberius ran for a second tribunate (which was not illegal, but unusual), tensions exploded.

Death of Tiberius

A group of senators led by **Scipio Nasica** confronted Tiberius and his supporters during an assembly on the Capitoline Hill. In the violence that followed, Tiberius and many of his followers were clubbed to death. It was the first time in the Republic's memory that a tribune had been killed by fellow Romans in a political dispute. Though the immediate crisis ended, Tiberius's murder showed a dark turn in Roman politics—physical violence was now a tool for handling disagreements.

Gaius Gracchus

Taking Up His Brother's Cause

Gaius Sempronius Gracchus, Tiberius's younger brother, came to prominence about a decade later. He was elected Tribune of the Plebs in 123 BC and again in 122 BC. Gaius was a skilled speaker who expanded on his brother's reforms, passing a wide range of laws aimed at helping the poor and curbing senatorial power.

Key Reforms of Gaius

1. **Land Distribution:** Gaius continued the work of the agrarian commission, giving more land to the poor.
2. **Grain Law:** He proposed selling grain to Roman citizens at a fixed, lower price. This provided some food security for the urban poor, though critics said it made them dependent on state handouts.
3. **Military Reforms:** Gaius tried to improve conditions for soldiers, such as providing state-funded equipment.
4. **Equestrian Class Empowerment:** Gaius passed laws that gave the **equites** (wealthy non-senators, often involved in business) control over certain courts dealing with provincial governors' corruption. This reduced the Senate's monopoly on judicial matters.

5. **Colonization Projects:** He wanted to found colonies overseas for Roman citizens, including one in Carthage's old territory, to relieve crowding in the city and give the poor new opportunities.

Senatus Consultum Ultimum and Gaius's Downfall

Wealthy senators felt threatened by Gaius's popularity. When he ran for a third tribunate and lost, they saw their chance. Another tribune moved to cancel Gaius's colonization plan. Violent clashes broke out between Gaius's supporters and opponents. Fearing a rebellion, the Senate issued the **Senatus Consultum Ultimum**—a decree giving consuls emergency power to "defend the Republic" by any means necessary.

Armed confrontations followed, and Gaius, realizing he was cornered, fled to the Aventine Hill, then to a grove across the Tiber. According to tradition, he ordered a slave to kill him rather than be captured. Over 3,000 of his followers were executed.

Thus ended the Gracchan reforms—at least in their most direct form. Yet the ideas they raised—land reform, fairer courts, and help for the poor—did not go away. Later leaders would revisit them, and the violence surrounding the Gracchi signaled a new era of political strife.

The Aftermath of the Gracchi

After Gaius's death in 121 BC, the Senate tried to roll back some of his reforms. Yet they could not entirely undo land distributions already granted. A generation of Roman citizens had seen the possibility of radical change—and how far the elite would go to stop it. Many small farmers did receive land, but the overall trend of latifundia expansion continued. Meanwhile, the problem of the urban poor remained.

Some moderate politicians tried to calm tensions. However, new issues—like the question of extending Roman citizenship to allied Italian communities—added more fuel to the fire. In the next decades, several reformers and generals rose to prominence, each with their own approach to Rome's social and economic crises.

Other Reform Attempts

Marcus Livius Drusus (the Younger)

In 91 BC, a tribune named **Marcus Livius Drusus** proposed a broad package of reforms, including cheap grain, land distributions, and the extension of Roman citizenship to all Italian allies. He hoped to unite various groups behind his plan. But powerful senators opposed him, and he was assassinated. This event triggered the **Social War**, as Italian allies demanded citizenship rights.

The Social War (91–88 BC)

Rome's Italian allies had long provided soldiers for Rome's armies but lacked a direct vote in Roman politics. They demanded citizenship. When Drusus's reforms failed, many Italian communities rebelled, forming their own confederation with a capital at Corfinium (renamed "Italia"). The **Social War** was brutal, but the Romans eventually won. However, as a concession, Rome granted **citizenship** to those Italians who remained loyal or laid down arms quickly. By the end of the war, most of Italy's free population became Roman citizens.

This major change addressed one key grievance but also swelled Rome's voting rolls. Now thousands more men had the right to vote in assemblies, though the actual process of voting still favored those who could travel to Rome easily. Nonetheless, the Social War was a turning point, mixing Italians and Romans into one political body.

Changing Power Dynamics

With more citizens, larger armies, and continuing land issues, Rome's politics grew more complicated. Senators competed with each other for prestige and wealth. Ambitious generals gained public favor by winning wars and promising benefits to veterans. More and more, violence seemed to loom over public life, as some leaders used intimidation to push their agendas.

Below, we highlight two big changes in how power was exercised:

1. **Rise of "New Men" (Nobiles vs. Novus Homo):** A **novus homo** (new man) was someone who achieved high office despite not coming from a famous political family. This trend allowed talented individuals from the equestrian or newly enfranchised classes to climb the ladder, challenging the old elite.
2. **Client Armies and Veterans:** Generals began promising land or wealth to their soldiers. Troops grew loyal to their commanders rather than to the state. This shift would later shake the Republic's foundations.

The Marian Reforms

One of the key figures who introduced major changes in the Roman army was **Gaius Marius**, a general and politician who rose from a relatively humble background. We will explore Marius in detail in Chapter 10. However, it is worth noting here that his military reforms—such as recruiting landless citizens and promising them a share of the spoils—helped transform the army into a professional force. This move addressed the problem of declining small farmers who traditionally formed the Roman legions, but it also made soldiers more dependent on their general's success.

Marius's success in wars against foreign enemies earned him repeated consulships, which was unusual and stirred controversy among the Senate. His story shows how social changes fed into the rise of strong individuals who reworked the Republic's rules.

Reform and Conservatism Clash

Even though the Gracchi and others tried to reform land ownership and help the poor, the wealthy senatorial class remained very powerful. Many senators argued that the old ways (the *mos maiorum*, or "custom of the ancestors") were best. They feared that reforms weakened the foundations of Rome by giving too much to the lower classes and empowering demagogues.

On the other side, reformers believed that ignoring poverty, landlessness, and corruption would tear the Republic apart from within. This divide did not vanish. Instead, it intensified, playing out in the assemblies and sometimes in street battles. By the early 1st century BC, Rome was a city filled with factions, each accusing the other of betraying the Republic.

Key Figures and Their Legacies

1. **Tiberius Gracchus:** Bold tribune who attempted land reforms; killed by senators, marking a new level of political violence.
2. **Gaius Gracchus:** Expanded reforms, gave more power to equites in courts, and tried to found colonies overseas. He too fell victim to senatorial opposition and was killed with many followers.
3. **Marcus Livius Drusus (the Younger):** Tried to solve multiple problems, including extending citizenship to Italians, but was assassinated, sparking the Social War.
4. **Gaius Marius:** A "new man" who would soon become one of Rome's most successful generals, leading to repeated consulships and a shift in how the army was recruited.

These individuals left a lasting impact. While their immediate reforms often failed or were rolled back, they exposed deep flaws in the Roman system—flaws that future leaders would exploit or try to fix.

The Widening Divide

By about 88 BC, the Republic stood on shaky ground:

- **Class Tensions:** Wealthy senators (the "optimates") resisted change, while populares (leaders appealing to the people) used tribunes and assemblies to push reforms.
- **Urban Unrest:** The city of Rome was crowded, with poor citizens sometimes rioting over grain prices or political disputes.
- **Military Dependence:** Armies were increasingly tied to individual generals, not the Senate as a whole.
- **Italian Allies Now Citizens:** The Social War ended, but the new citizens across Italy changed voting patterns and political alliances.

These conditions were ripe for a strong leader to step in with promises of order, wealth, and glory. The door was open for generals who could command loyal troops to bypass or reshape the existing political structures.

CHAPTER 10

THE RISE OF STRONG GENERALS

Introduction to a New Era

By the late 2nd and early 1st century BC, the Roman Republic was under strain. Land conflicts, poverty among the masses, and fights over citizenship had left deep scars on Rome's political life. A series of wars—some external, some internal—allowed ambitious generals to gain unprecedented power. They found support among soldiers who were more loyal to their commanders than to the Senate.

This chapter explores how **Gaius Marius**, **Lucius Cornelius Sulla**, and later figures like **Gnaeus Pompeius Magnus** (Pompey) and **Marcus Licinius Crassus** rose to prominence. We will see how military victories brought them wealth and influence, setting the stage for civil strife. By the end of this chapter, the Republic itself would tremble as armies led by Roman citizens fought one another.

Gaius Marius: The People's General

Early Career and "New Man" Status

Gaius Marius (157–86 BC) was born near Arpinum, a town outside Rome, to an equestrian family with no great political heritage. He was a true **novus homo**, or "new man"—someone who rose to high office without noble ancestry. Marius made his name as a soldier, serving under Scipio Aemilianus in the Numantine War (in Spain). Through grit and skill, Marius won recognition, married into the patrician Julia family (related to Julius Caesar's clan), and eventually ran for political office.

The Jugurthine War (112–105 BC)

In the late 2nd century BC, trouble brewed in Numidia (North Africa). **King Jugurtha**, a cunning ruler, bribed Roman officials and defied the Republic's authority. The Senate sent armies, but they failed repeatedly—allegedly due to corruption or poor leadership. Marius, elected consul in 107 BC, took command. He reformed the army by accepting **volunteers** from among the poor and giving them training and hope for land. His soldiers were fiercely loyal to him.

Marius, aided by his energetic quaestor **Lucius Cornelius Sulla**, captured Jugurtha. The war ended with Jugurtha paraded in Marius's triumph. Marius gained enormous popularity as the man who defeated Rome's African foe while cleaning up senatorial corruption.

The Cimbric and Teutonic Threat

Almost immediately, Rome faced a new danger from Germanic tribes: the **Cimbri** and the **Teutones**. These groups migrated south, threatening Gaul (modern France) and northern Italy. Several Roman armies were destroyed. The panicked Senate turned to Marius, electing him consul year after year—a big break from tradition (he held consulship seven times in total).

Marius reorganized the legions, training recruits intensively and improving discipline. He introduced the concept of **cohorts**, larger units than the old maniples, simplifying command. He also encouraged loyalty by promising land and spoils. In 102 BC, Marius crushed the Teutones at **Aquae Sextiae** (in southern Gaul). In 101 BC, he joined another consul to defeat the Cimbri at **Vercellae** in northern Italy. These victories saved Rome from a northern invasion. Marius was hailed as the "third founder of Rome," a national hero.

Marius's Political Legacy

Despite his military success, Marius struggled with politics. He supported popular measures and allied with tribunes who pushed for land distributions to his veterans. But he lacked the finesse to navigate senatorial politics peacefully. As tensions flared, Marius eventually withdrew from public life, though events soon dragged him back. His rivalry with a former subordinate, **Sulla**, would shape Rome's future.

Lucius Cornelius Sulla: From Lieutenant to Rival

Sulla's Rise

Lucius Cornelius Sulla (138–78 BC) was born into an old patrician family that had fallen on hard times. He served under Marius in the Jugurthine War, playing a key role in capturing King Jugurtha. Later, he distinguished himself in wars against Germanic tribes and gained wealth by inheritance. He had a flamboyant lifestyle but proved to be a ruthless and efficient commander.

The Social War and Sulla's Consulship

When the **Social War** (91–88 BC) broke out, Sulla fought bravely against the Italian rebels. He won several victories, boosting his reputation. By 88 BC, he was elected **consul**. Meanwhile, Marius was older but still influential, and he envied Sulla's successes.

That same year, a conflict arose over who would lead a war against **King Mithridates** of Pontus in Asia Minor. The Senate gave the command to Sulla, but Marius maneuvered in the assemblies to get it reassigned to himself. Outraged, Sulla did the unthinkable—he marched his army on Rome, forcing Marius to flee. This shocking act was the first time a Roman general used his troops to seize control of the city.

Sulla's First March on Rome

Breaking Republican Norms

Sulla's decision to march on Rome shattered the long-standing rule that soldiers were not to enter the city in arms. But Sulla believed he had no choice if he wanted to keep his command and defend his dignity. Once in Rome, he declared Marius and his allies outlaws. After ensuring his appointment was secure, Sulla left to fight Mithridates.

Marius Returns

With Sulla gone, Marius returned from exile. He and his ally **Cinna** seized Rome themselves, killing or driving out Sulla's supporters. Marius was elected consul again in 86 BC, though he died soon afterward. Cinna continued ruling Rome, but the city braced for Sulla's return. This back-and-forth occupation signaled the start of **civil war**, even though it was not yet official.

The Mithridatic Wars

While Rome was in turmoil, **Mithridates VI** of Pontus took advantage of the chaos. He invaded Roman provinces in Asia Minor and allegedly orchestrated the massacre of thousands of Roman and Italian residents there. Sulla, now in Greece and Asia Minor, campaigned against Mithridates successfully, winning battles and forcing him to retreat.

In 85 BC, Sulla made peace with Mithridates, letting him keep part of his kingdom but paying an indemnity and surrendering ships. Sulla's priority was returning to Italy to face the political crisis. Many Romans disliked the generous terms, but Sulla wanted a quick settlement to save his position in Rome.

Sulla's Second March on Rome and Dictatorship

Civil War Erupts

In 83 BC, Sulla landed in southern Italy with his legions. Loyal forces of Cinna tried to stop him, but Sulla proved too strong. He defeated several armies, forging alliances with individuals like **Pompey**, a young general who would later become famous. By 82 BC, Sulla was the master of Rome again.

Proscriptions

To eliminate opposition, Sulla published **proscriptions**—lists of enemies of the state who could be killed on sight, with rewards offered. Their property was confiscated. This reign of terror allowed Sulla to get rid of rivals and enrich his supporters. Many old families lost their fortunes, while ambitious men profited. It was one of the darkest chapters of Roman violence.

Sulla as Dictator

The Senate appointed Sulla as **dictator** without a time limit to "restore the Republic." He passed numerous reforms intended to strengthen the Senate and reduce the power of tribunes. For instance, he removed the tribunes' ability to propose legislation freely and made it harder for men to climb the political ladder too quickly. His aim was to stabilize the Republic under senatorial control.

Sulla's Resignation and Death

In 79 BC, to the surprise of many, Sulla resigned his dictatorship and retired to his villa. He claimed he had done his job. He even walked around Rome without a guard, boasting that no one dared harm him. He died of illness in 78 BC. While his reforms temporarily boosted the Senate's power, they did not solve the underlying social issues. If anything, Sulla's example showed that a determined general could dominate Rome by force.

After Sulla: New Power Players

With Sulla gone, the stage was open for a new generation of powerful leaders. Two men who had helped Sulla rose quickly: **Pompey** and **Crassus**.

Pompey the Great

Gnaeus Pompeius Magnus—Pompey—was born around 106 BC. He was from a wealthy Italian family and gained fame by raising his own troops to support Sulla. After Sulla's victory, Pompey fought rebellious generals in Africa and Spain, earning the nickname "Magnus" (the Great). He celebrated multiple triumphs and was popular with both soldiers and the public.

Marcus Licinius Crassus

Crassus was known for his vast wealth, much of it acquired through property speculation, including buying estates from proscribed individuals at low prices. He also proved a capable commander, notably defeating the slave revolt led by **Spartacus** (73–71 BC). However, Crassus always craved more recognition—he wanted the military glory that Pompey and others had achieved in foreign wars.

The Revolt of Spartacus

Between 73 and 71 BC, a group of gladiators led by **Spartacus** started a major slave revolt in Italy. They won several battles, causing panic in Rome. Crassus was given the task of crushing the revolt. He managed to corner and defeat the rebels. Pompey arrived from Spain and mopped up the remainder, claiming partial credit. Both Crassus and Pompey used their success to gain consulships in 70 BC, ignoring Sulla's rules about age and political steps. During their joint consulship, they reversed some of Sulla's reforms and restored power to the tribunes.

Changing Alliances and Ambitions

Pompey's Campaigns in the East

From 67 to 62 BC, Pompey gained extraordinary commands to deal with pirates in the Mediterranean and then to finish off the war against King Mithridates. He swiftly cleared the pirates from the seas by reorganizing naval squadrons. Next, he defeated Mithridates in Asia Minor, then expanded Roman control into Syria and parts of Judea. These actions made him wildly famous and wealthy. He also set up client kingdoms, further increasing Rome's eastern territories.

When he returned to Rome in 62 BC, Pompey sought land for his veterans and ratification of his eastern settlements. However, the Senate, jealous of his power, dragged its feet.

Crassus's Desire for Military Glory

Crassus, overshadowed by Pompey's triumphs, yearned to prove himself in a grand foreign war. He was an expert in finance but lacked the heroic general reputation that Pompey and others enjoyed. He would later seek a chance to wage war in the East, leading to a tragic outcome (the Battle of Carrhae in 53 BC, beyond our current scope).

The Rise of Julius Caesar

During this time, a younger politician named **Julius Caesar** also gained attention, partly because of his Marian connections (his aunt was Marius's wife). Caesar allied himself with Pompey and Crassus, forming the **First Triumvirate** in 60 BC. This alliance let them bypass senatorial opposition to achieve their goals: Pompey got land for his veterans, Crassus pursued financial legislation, and Caesar became consul and then governor of Gaul.

Although we will discuss Caesar in more detail later, his rise belongs to the pattern: popular generals who used alliances, wealth, and soldiers' loyalty to shape the Republic's future.

Shifts in the Republic's Structure

By the mid-1st century BC, the old balance in Rome was changed:

1. **Weakened Senate:** Generals like Marius, Sulla, and Pompey proved they could override or manipulate the Senate with armed force or popular support.
2. **Dependence on Generals:** Large armies of professional soldiers became loyal to commanders who promised spoils and land, not to the Senate or the Republic.
3. **Class Divisions Remained:** Despite certain reforms, latifundia thrived, and slave labor was widespread. The urban poor still needed grain distributions and struggled to find stable work.

4. **Political Coalitions:** Alliances like the First Triumvirate let powerful men combine forces, outmaneuvering rivals. This was a new form of politics, steering the Republic without formal offices at times.

All these trends foreshadowed the final collapse of the Republic's traditional system. Rivalries among strong leaders would soon erupt into civil wars, culminating in the rise of **Imperial Rome**.

Chapter 10 Summary

1. **Marius's Military Reforms:** Gaius Marius opened the army to landless citizens, won major wars (Jugurthine, against the Cimbri and Teutones), and was elected consul multiple times. This transformed soldiers' loyalty toward their general.
2. **Sulla's Seizure of Power:** Lucius Cornelius Sulla marched on Rome to secure his command against Mithridates, defeating Marius's faction. He became dictator, instituted proscriptions, and temporarily boosted the Senate's authority.
3. **Pompey and Crassus:** After Sulla's death, these two men rose by defeating threats like Spartacus's slave revolt and waging successful campaigns in Spain and the East. Their rivalry and desire for recognition shaped Roman politics.
4. **First Triumvirate Seeds:** Pompey's frustration with the Senate, Crassus's ambition, and Julius Caesar's cunning led to an informal alliance that bypassed traditional power structures.
5. **Changing Republic:** Armies now belonged to generals, not the state. Political violence, internal distrust, and personal ambition set the stage for the Republic's final struggles.

CHAPTER 11

THE END OF THE REPUBLIC

Tensions Boil Over

In the previous chapter, we saw how generals like Gaius Marius, Lucius Cornelius Sulla, Pompey, and Crassus used their armies and popularity to gain influence in the Roman Republic. Their actions weakened the Senate's authority, and political violence became more common. By the mid-1st century BC, it was clear that the old republic was under strain. Rome's empire had grown too large, and its government system had not kept pace. Factions formed, alliances shifted, and powerful men fought for control.

In this chapter, we focus on the final decades of the Roman Republic. We will see how **Julius Caesar**, **Pompey**, and **Crassus** formed the **First Triumvirate**, and how Caesar's growing power led to a devastating civil war. We will also learn about Caesar's dictatorship, his assassination, and the resulting power struggle that ended with **Octavian**—later known as Augustus—emerging victorious. By the end of this period, the Roman Republic had collapsed, giving way to a new system of rule.

The First Triumvirate

Caesar's Beginnings

Gaius Julius Caesar was born around 100 BC to a patrician family related to Marius by marriage. During Sulla's dominance, Caesar faced danger but survived, partly through the help of friends and partly by keeping a low profile. Over time, he proved to be an excellent speaker, a clever politician, and a bold military commander.

In the 60s BC, Caesar held several offices: quaestor, aedile, and pontifex maximus (chief priest). Each position expanded his influence. He spent lavishly on public games and buildings, earning popularity with the people. Like many ambitious Romans, he sought the consulship, but the Senate was often suspicious of him, seeing him as a *populares* leader who catered to the commoners.

Caesar, Pompey, and Crassus Join Forces

Pompey and Crassus were already powerful. Pompey had just returned from his campaigns in the East and needed the Senate to approve land for his veterans and confirm his arrangements in conquered territories. Crassus, the wealthiest man in Rome, wanted laws favoring his business interests and another chance to win military glory.

All three men found the Senate uncooperative. In 60 BC, they formed an informal alliance later called the **First Triumvirate**: **Caesar**, **Pompey**, and **Crassus**. Each promised to help the others achieve their goals. Caesar would run for consul in 59 BC, backing Pompey's land bill for his veterans, while Crassus would get financial reforms. Pompey and Crassus, in turn, would help Caesar gain the governorship of important provinces.

Caesar's Consulship (59 BC)

As consul in 59 BC, Caesar pushed through legislation granting farmland to Pompey's soldiers. He also passed laws beneficial to Crassus. The Senate opposed him fiercely, so Caesar often relied on the people's assembly, using Pompey's veterans in Rome to pressure opponents. His co-consul, Marcus Bibulus, tried to resist but was bullied and effectively sidelined. Romans joked that the year was "the consulship of Julius and Caesar," since Bibulus had little power.

At the end of his term, Caesar secured a **proconsul** position over **Cisalpine Gaul** (northern Italy) and **Transalpine Gaul** (southern France). The Senate, hoping to keep him out of Rome, gave him this governorship. They did not expect what Caesar would do next.

Caesar's Gallic Wars

Conquest of Gaul

From 58 BC to 50 BC, Caesar waged campaigns in **Gaul** (roughly modern France, Belgium, and parts of Switzerland and Germany). He claimed to be defending Roman allies from hostile tribes. In truth, he aimed to expand Rome's territory and enhance his own reputation. Over several years, he defeated powerful tribes like the Helvetii, Suebi, and the Belgae. He even made expeditions across the **Rhine River** and into **Britain** (in 55 and 54 BC), although he did not establish permanent rule there.

Caesar's victories were stunning. He wrote commentaries—*Commentarii de Bello Gallico*—describing his campaigns. These writings spread in Rome, glorifying his achievements and showing him as a great hero. The wealth he gained from Gaul funded public works and bribes back in Rome, maintaining his popularity and influence.

Problems for the Triumvirate

While Caesar was in Gaul, the other two triumvirs faced troubles.

- **Pompey** stayed in Rome, gaining more prestige but clashing with political opponents. He grew closer to conservative senators, stepping away from Caesar's radical style.
- **Crassus** went east seeking military glory in a war against the Parthian Empire. In 53 BC, he was defeated and killed at the **Battle of Carrhae**—a massive blow to Rome's pride and to the Triumvirate's balance of power.

With Crassus gone, the alliance was fragile. Pompey's wife, Julia—Caesar's daughter—died in 54 BC, removing another link between the two men. Slowly, Pompey and Caesar drifted apart, each suspicious of the other's intentions.

Rising Tensions with Pompey

The Senate's Fear

As Caesar's fame in Gaul grew, many senators worried he would march on Rome when his proconsulship ended. They demanded that Caesar disband his army and return to Rome as a private citizen if he wanted to run for consul again. Caesar refused, fearing that once he was without troops, his enemies would put him on trial or even harm him.

Pompey's Shift

Pompey, once Caesar's ally, aligned himself with the Senate. In 52 BC, he became sole consul after political violence erupted in the streets, and he took steps to limit Caesar's influence. Seeing Caesar as too powerful and ambitious, Pompey accepted the Senate's orders that Caesar must lay down his command.

This stalemate led to a final confrontation. Caesar argued that he should be allowed to keep his imperium until he could stand for consul, just as Pompey had once done. The Senate refused. In January 49 BC, they passed a decree ordering Caesar to disarm. He had to choose between surrendering or fighting.

Caesar Crosses the Rubicon

"The die is cast." So legend says Caesar declared when he made his fateful decision: he led his troops across the **Rubicon River**, the boundary between his province and Italy, violating Roman law forbidding a general to enter Italy with an army. This event in 49 BC sparked civil war. Caesar's crossing meant he was rebelling against the Senate and Pompey.

With surprising speed, Caesar advanced on Rome. Pompey and many senators fled to Greece, believing they could raise a massive army to defeat Caesar. Meanwhile, Caesar moved quickly through Italy, encountering little resistance. He aimed to settle the war fast, but Pompey and his allies refused to negotiate, hoping to regroup abroad.

The Civil War Begins

Battles in Spain and Greece

First, Caesar went to **Hispania** (Spain), where Pompey's legates controlled strong forces. Caesar overcame them swiftly. Returning to Rome, he took the treasury to fund his campaigns. Then he sailed east to face Pompey directly.

In 48 BC, Caesar and Pompey clashed in several engagements, with the pivotal battle at **Pharsalus** in central Greece. Despite being outnumbered, Caesar's veterans fought well. Pompey's larger army collapsed, and he fled the battlefield.

Pompey's Fate

Pompey escaped to Egypt, hoping for help from the young Pharaoh **Ptolemy XIII**. Instead, Ptolemy's advisers, hoping to please Caesar, murdered Pompey upon his arrival. They sent Pompey's severed head to Caesar. Caesar was reportedly upset by this deed, as Pompey had once been his son-in-law and fellow consul. Pompey's violent end marked the fall of one of Rome's greatest generals.

Caesar in Egypt

After Pompey's death, Caesar arrived in Egypt and became embroiled in the country's royal family feud. **Cleopatra VII**, sister and co-ruler to Ptolemy XIII, sought Caesar's support. He helped Cleopatra defeat her brother, and the two became allies—some say lovers. Cleopatra later bore a son named Caesarion.

Caesar lingered in Egypt for a time, enjoying Cleopatra's court. Many Romans criticized him for staying away from pressing matters in Rome. However, Caesar's involvement in Egyptian affairs strengthened Rome's influence over the Nile region and made Cleopatra a famous figure in Roman politics.

The Last Conflicts

In the next two years, Caesar traveled throughout the eastern Mediterranean, settling disputes and defeating remaining enemies:

- **Pharnaces** (son of Mithridates) in Asia Minor: Caesar's swift victory led him to declare "Veni, Vidi, Vici" (I came, I saw, I conquered).
- In **Africa**, he beat the last Pompeian forces at **Thapsus** (46 BC).
- In **Hispania**, he crushed Pompey's sons at **Munda** (45 BC).

By 45 BC, Caesar was the undisputed master of the Roman world. He returned to Rome, where he was named **dictator for life** (*dictator perpetuo*). This marked a dramatic change: no Roman in living memory had held such power for an indefinite term.

Caesar's Reforms and Ambitions

Back in Rome, Caesar launched many reforms:

1. **Calendar Reform:** He introduced the **Julian calendar**, aligning it with the solar year. This new system, with 365 days and a leap day every four years, replaced the old, confusing lunar calendar.
2. **Colonies for Veterans and Poor Citizens:** He founded colonies overseas, giving land to veterans and the urban poor.
3. **Senate Expansion:** To weaken the Senate's old guard, he added many new members, including non-Italians from Gaul and Spain.
4. **Debt and Tax Reforms:** He tried to reduce debt burdens and curb tax-farming abuses in the provinces.

Caesar also showed signs of wanting more than just a dictatorship. Statues of him were placed across the city, and people worried he might declare himself a king. While some adored him, others saw his power as a threat to republican freedoms.

The Ides of March

Caesar's Growing Power

By early 44 BC, Caesar's position seemed unassailable. He was dictator for life, had reformed many aspects of Roman governance, and was beloved by the common people for providing grain, public celebrations, and colonization opportunities. However, senators who cherished the republic's traditions felt he had gone too far. Some suspected he wanted a royal title.

One day, at a festival, someone placed a diadem (a symbol of kingship) on Caesar's head. He refused it, but rumors spread that he had staged the act to test how the people would react. He also wore a special purple robe at public events—another sign resembling a king's garb. No matter his true intentions, the idea of a single monarch ruling Rome alarmed many senators.

The Conspirators

A group of about 60 senators began plotting Caesar's assassination. Key figures included **Gaius Cassius Longinus** and **Marcus Junius Brutus** (descendant of the famous Lucius Junius Brutus who had overthrown the last king of Rome). They believed killing Caesar was the only way to save the republic from monarchy. Some conspirators acted out of genuine fear for liberty; others may have been motivated by jealousy or loss of status.

March 15, 44 BC

The plotters chose the **Ides of March** (March 15th) to strike. Caesar arrived at the **Theater of Pompey** for a Senate meeting. Inside a hall known as the **Curia Pompeia**, the conspirators surrounded him. According to stories, Caesar was stabbed multiple times, with Brutus among the attackers. Caesar reportedly said, "Et tu, Brute?" ("You too, Brutus?") or something similar in shock. He died at the foot of Pompey's statue, ironically beneath the image of his former rival.

This assassination rocked Rome. The conspirators rushed into the streets shouting that they had saved the republic. But instead of receiving applause, they faced confusion and fear. The common people did not hail them as heroes. Many were angered by Caesar's murder, as he had been popular for his generosity.

The Aftermath and the Second Triumvirate

Chaos in Rome

Right after Caesar's death, the city was thrown into uncertainty. The conspirators tried to calm the crowds, promising a return to republican rule. But Caesar's supporters were outraged. A funeral was held in the Forum, and Caesar's ally **Mark Antony** delivered a stirring speech. Antony read Caesar's will, which left money to every Roman citizen and bequeathed his gardens to the people. The crowd turned into a mob, burning the conspirators' houses and forcing them to flee.

Antony, Lepidus, and Octavian

Three main figures emerged to fill the power vacuum:

1. **Mark Antony (Marcus Antonius):** A loyal friend of Caesar, known for his bravery in battle and his ability to rally the masses. He initially took control of Caesar's funds and documents.
2. **Marcus Aemilius Lepidus:** Another ally of Caesar, who had a strong following among certain army units and controlled important positions in the city.
3. **Gaius Octavius (Octavian):** Caesar's 18-year-old grandnephew, named in Caesar's will as his adopted son and main heir. People were surprised by Caesar's choice—Octavian was young and untested, but he now had Caesar's name (Gaius Julius Caesar Octavianus) and a claim to Caesar's legacy.

These three men formed the **Second Triumvirate** in 43 BC through the "Lex Titia," giving themselves almost unlimited power to punish Caesar's killers and reorganize the Republic.

Proscriptions and Philippi

Crushing the Conspirators

Like Sulla before them, the Second Triumvirate used **proscriptions** to eliminate enemies and raise money by seizing their property. Many senators and equites were killed or exiled. One famous victim was **Cicero**, the great orator, who had criticized Antony.

The Triumvirs then went east to confront **Brutus** and **Cassius**, who had raised armies in Macedonia and Asia Minor. The resulting battles at **Philippi** in 42 BC were decisive. Antony and Octavian (though Octavian was sick during much of the fighting) defeated the conspirators. Brutus and Cassius took their own lives rather than face capture.

With the conspirators dead, the Triumvirs believed they were avenging Caesar. But peace did not last.

Division of Power

After Philippi, the triumvirs split the empire among themselves:

- Antony took the East (Greece, Asia Minor, and Egypt).
- Octavian took Italy and the western provinces (Gaul, Spain, and possibly parts of Africa).
- Lepidus was given Africa (though his role was soon overshadowed).

Tensions grew, especially between Octavian and Antony. Both wanted supreme authority. Lepidus, lacking real power, would fade into the background.

Antony and Cleopatra

Antony's Alliance with Cleopatra

In the East, Antony sought funds and support. He summoned **Cleopatra VII** of Egypt, who had been Caesar's companion. Cleopatra sailed up the **Cydnus River** in a lavish barge, impressing Antony. They soon became lovers. Cleopatra provided him with money and troops, hoping that with Antony's help, she could maintain Egypt's independence and even expand her influence.

Antony divorced **Octavia**, Octavian's sister, and lived with Cleopatra. This angered many Romans, who felt Antony betrayed Roman customs. Rumors spread that Antony planned to give Roman territories to Cleopatra and their children, undermining Roman authority.

Octavian's Propaganda

In Rome, Octavian used the scandal to turn public opinion against Antony. He presented himself as the champion of traditional Roman values, while painting Antony as the puppet of a foreign queen. The Senate, alarmed by Antony's behavior, supported Octavian. By 32 BC, both sides prepared for war.

The Final War of the Republic

Battle of Actium (31 BC)

Antony and Cleopatra assembled a large fleet in Greece. Octavian's admiral, **Marcus Agrippa**, blockaded them. On September 2, 31 BC, at the **Battle of Actium**, Antony tried to break out to sea. In the midst of battle, Cleopatra's ships retreated, and Antony followed, leaving much of his fleet to surrender. This defeat effectively ended Antony's hopes.

Antony and Cleopatra's Deaths

Antony and Cleopatra fled to Egypt, with Octavian close behind. In 30 BC, as Octavian's forces approached Alexandria, Antony, hearing false news that Cleopatra was dead, fell on his sword. Cleopatra, refusing to be paraded in a Roman triumph, took her own life—according to legend, by asp bite. With their deaths, Egypt became another Roman province, and the last major rival to Octavian was gone.

Octavian's Triumph

Octavian now stood as the sole ruler of Rome. In 29 BC, he returned to a hero's welcome, celebrating a grand triumph. The civil wars that had raged on and off for nearly two decades were finally over.

The **Roman Republic**, exhausted by internal conflicts, had fallen. Octavian was only 32 years old but commanded an empire stretching from Spain to Syria, Britain's shores to North Africa's deserts. He promised to restore peace and preserve the old forms of government, but in reality, power was concentrated in his hands.

CHAPTER 12

THE AGE OF AUGUSTUS

A New Chapter Begins

At the end of Chapter 11, **Octavian** stood alone as Rome's master, having defeated Antony and Cleopatra. The civil wars were over, and the Roman world was finally at peace. Yet the people were wary: they had seen strong men seize power before—Marius, Sulla, and Julius Caesar—only to bring more violence. Octavian needed a lasting solution, one that satisfied both the Senate and the masses.

In this chapter, we examine how Octavian carefully formed a new system called the **Principate**, taking the title **Augustus** and ruling as Rome's first emperor (though he never openly claimed to be a king or dictator). We will see how he balanced old republican traditions with the reality of his supreme power, ushering in a long period of stability and prosperity known as the **Pax Romana**.

The "Restoration" of the Republic

Octavian's Careful Approach

Octavian returned to Rome in 29 BC, celebrating a grand triple triumph. Over the next few years, he presented himself as the **restorer of peace**. He demobilized many soldiers, giving them land. He also acted humble in public, wearing simple clothes and speaking modestly, to avoid Caesar's fate of seeming too proud or "kingly."

In 27 BC, Octavian made a formal show of returning full power to the Senate and the people. The Senate, grateful for peace, "begged" him to keep control. They awarded him the title **Augustus** ("the revered one"), signifying his special status. Augustus also took the honorific **Princeps** ("first citizen"), instead of a kingly or dictatorial title. This arrangement formed the basis of the **Principate**—a system where the emperor held ultimate authority but pretended to uphold republican traditions.

Titles and Powers

Under the Principate, Augustus gathered many powers:

- **Imperium proconsulare**: Control over key provinces with most of the army stationed there.
- **Tribunicia potestas**: The legal powers of a tribune, such as vetoing laws and calling the assembly.
- **Pontifex Maximus**: Chief priest, overseeing Roman religion.

He also used the Senate to pass laws he favored. Though the Senate still existed, it rarely opposed Augustus. In effect, the republic's offices—consuls, tribunes, censors—carried on, but real authority resided with Augustus.

The Pax Romana Begins

With the civil wars concluded, Rome entered a period of relative peace and stability that would last about two centuries. Historians call this the **Pax Romana** (Roman Peace).

Military Reorganization

Augustus restructured the army, keeping about 28 legions of professional soldiers. Veterans stayed loyal for a fixed term (usually around 20 years) and then received pensions or land. This standing army was stationed at the frontiers, ready to defend or expand Rome's borders. He also created the **Praetorian Guard**, an elite unit based in or near Rome to protect the emperor and maintain order.

Administrative Changes

To rule the vast empire effectively, Augustus divided provinces into two types:

1. **Imperial Provinces:** Controlled by Augustus directly through his legates (legati), usually where legions were stationed.
2. **Senatorial Provinces:** Governed by proconsuls chosen by the Senate, typically peaceful areas without a large military presence.

He also organized a professional civil service, employing freedmen and equestrians (wealthy non-senators) to handle tasks like tax collection and record-keeping. This more efficient administration meant fewer abuses and a more reliable flow of taxes and supplies.

Public Works and Morale

Augustus famously boasted that he found Rome a city of brick and left it a city of marble. He built or restored temples, forums, theaters, roads, and aqueducts. He also sponsored games and festivals to entertain the populace. These projects provided jobs, beautified the city, and reinforced Augustus's image as a benevolent ruler.

Moral and Social Reforms

Augustus saw himself not just as a political leader but as a guardian of Roman morals and religion. He believed the civil wars had been a punishment for Rome's moral decline.

Marriage and Family Laws

He passed laws encouraging marriage, penalizing adultery, and rewarding families with children. The goal was to boost the birth rate among upper-class Romans and revive traditional values. Some found these laws invasive, but they reflected Augustus's desire for a stable society with strong family units.

Religious Revival

Augustus restored many temples and revived old religious ceremonies. He revived the **ludi saeculares** (Secular Games) and other festivals to honor the gods. As **Pontifex Maximus**, he appointed priests and supervised religious life closely. He also promoted worship of his **"genius"** or spirit, which gradually led to the **imperial cult**, where emperors were honored (and sometimes deified) after death.

Literature and the Arts

This period saw a flourishing of Latin literature. **Virgil** composed the **Aeneid**, linking Rome's founding to the Trojan hero Aeneas and praising the new age under Augustus. **Horace**, **Livy**, and **Ovid** also wrote works reflecting Rome's history, moral values, and culture. Wealthy patrons, including Augustus and his friend Maecenas, supported these poets. Architecture, sculpture, and other arts also thrived, often glorifying the emperor and Roman achievements.

Expanding the Empire

Conquests and Boundaries

Augustus sought to secure Rome's frontiers rather than conquer indefinitely. However, he did add new regions:

- **Egypt**: Already annexed by Octavian in 30 BC, it became his personal province, providing huge grain supplies.
- **Galatia**: In Asia Minor, turned into a Roman province.
- **Raetia and Noricum**: In the Alpine regions, helping protect Italy.
- **Pannonia and Moesia**: Along the Danube, providing a frontier against tribes from the north.

He also tried to push Rome's boundary to the **Elbe River** in Germany, but the **Battle of the Teutoburg Forest** in AD 9 ended that ambition when Germanic tribes ambushed and destroyed three Roman legions. This defeat deeply troubled Augustus, who reportedly lamented, "Varus, give me back my legions!" Afterward, Rome set the **Rhine** as its main frontier in the north.

Diplomacy and Client States

Augustus used diplomacy, encouraging local kings to become "friends of Rome" in places like the eastern provinces. This approach fostered stability without direct occupation. Client kingdoms sent tribute and recognized Roman leadership. If they rebelled, Roman legions were ready to step in.

Family and Succession Problems

Augustus's Heirs

One of Augustus's main worries was who would succeed him. As he claimed not to be a king, he could not simply declare an heir. Yet the empire needed continuity. Augustus tried to groom male relatives: his nephew Marcellus, his friend and general Agrippa, and then Agrippa's sons by Augustus's daughter Julia. Tragedy struck when several died young, forcing Augustus to change plans.

Finally, he adopted **Tiberius**, his stepson from his marriage to Livia Drusilla. Tiberius was an experienced general but not very popular in Rome. Nonetheless, he was the only viable option left, so Augustus gradually transferred powers to him to ensure stability.

The Fate of Julia

Augustus's only child, **Julia**, married Marcellus, then Agrippa, and then Tiberius. She became a central piece in Augustus's succession puzzle. However, she was later accused of adultery and banished, reflecting Augustus's strict moral codes. This personal scandal showed how hard it was for the imperial family to live under the moral standards Augustus set for the entire society.

Late Reign and Governance

The Principate Matures

As Augustus aged, he increased the size of the Senate and appointed new senators from across Italy and the provinces to ensure loyalty. The old aristocracy had mostly adapted to the new regime, realizing that cooperation with Augustus was the only path to influence.

Elders in the Senate continued formal debates, but Augustus often guided decisions from behind the scenes. He also created permanent administrative offices to handle grain distribution, fire services, and city upkeep, improving daily life in Rome.

Praetorian Guard's Role

The **Praetorian Guard**, originally formed to protect the emperor, expanded in size and influence. Commanded by a **Praetorian Prefect**, this elite unit could sway politics by controlling access to the emperor. Over time, the Guard became a key factor in choosing or deposing emperors, though under Augustus it mostly stayed loyal.

The Empire's Prosperity and Challenges

Economic Growth

With peace restored and secure trade routes, Rome's economy flourished. Roads, canals, and sea lanes carried goods from all corners of the empire to the capital. Grain from Egypt, olive oil from Africa and Spain, spices and silk from the East—the variety was immense. Cities like Carthage, Antioch, and Alexandria thrived as commercial hubs.

Coinage was standardized, helping commerce. Augustus minted coins bearing his image and titles, spreading his authority and propaganda throughout the provinces.

Frontier Pressures

Despite the Pax Romana, Rome constantly monitored frontier threats. Germanic tribes tested the Rhine border, and steppe peoples like the Sarmatians and Roxolani roamed near the Danube. In the East, the Parthian Empire remained a rival, though Augustus negotiated for the return of Roman standards lost by Crassus at Carrhae.

While Augustus preferred diplomacy, he sometimes used force if negotiations failed. However, unlike some Roman leaders, he aimed to consolidate rather than endlessly expand, hoping stable borders would produce lasting peace.

Cultural Flourishing

Literature and Philosophy

We already mentioned **Virgil's Aeneid**, which glorified Roman destiny and Augustus's role. **Horace** wrote odes praising simple

Roman virtues. **Livy** compiled a huge history of Rome, from its mythical origins to his own day, highlighting the city's moral lessons. **Ovid** explored love and mythology in his poetry, though he fell out of favor with Augustus and was exiled.

Philosophical schools like Stoicism and Epicureanism attracted Roman elites, teaching self-control and reason. Many Romans combined these ideas with their own religious traditions, creating a rich intellectual scene.

Architecture and Art

Augustus promoted a grand building program. The **Ara Pacis** (Altar of Peace) celebrated the Pax Romana, featuring reliefs of the imperial family and religious scenes. Triumphal arches and statues honored victories, while new roads linked distant provinces. Roman cities took on a more unified look, featuring forums, amphitheaters, and bathhouses modeled after the capital.

Augustus's Death and Legacy

The Final Years

By AD 14, Augustus was in his mid-70s. He had ruled for over 40 years, longer than most Romans had ever experienced one ruler in their lifetime. He spent his final months ensuring Tiberius would smoothly succeed him. He wrote a personal summary of his achievements, the **Res Gestae Divi Augusti** ("The Deeds of the Divine Augustus"), to be inscribed publicly after his death, boasting of his building projects, victories, and gifts to the people.

Passing of the First Emperor

Augustus died on August 19, AD 14, at Nola in Campania. According to tradition, Livia and Tiberius were with him. The Senate declared him a **god** (*Divus Augustus*). Tiberius became the new princeps, following the system Augustus created. The empire mourned a man who, despite flaws and controversies, ended a century of civil wars and laid the foundation for a stable empire.

Lasting Influence

Augustus's Principate shaped Roman history for centuries. Future emperors kept the title "Augustus," and the empire's governance followed the patterns he set. The Pax Romana he began allowed art, commerce, and culture to thrive. Even after the empire eventually faced crises, Augustus's reign stood as a golden age in Roman memory.

CHAPTER 13

THE EARLY EMPERORS

The Julio-Claudian Dynasty Begins

In the previous chapter, we saw how **Augustus** established the Principate, a system blending the old Republic's structures with the reality of one-man rule. After Augustus died in AD 14, his stepson, **Tiberius**, took over as princeps (emperor). Tiberius was the first of a series of rulers from Augustus's family, often called the **Julio-Claudian dynasty**. These emperors—Tiberius, Caligula, Claudius, and Nero—shared connections by blood or adoption, continuing the line begun by Julius Caesar and Augustus.

This chapter looks at the early emperors who followed Augustus, then carries us through a turbulent period that included emperors from the Flavian dynasty. We will see that some of these rulers maintained stability and accomplished much for Rome, while others became infamous for cruelty and excess. By the end, the stage is set for a new golden era under the "Five Good Emperors."

Tiberius (AD 14–37)

Reluctant Heir

When Augustus died, **Tiberius** was about 55 years old. He was an experienced general and statesman, but he had a sober, reserved personality. Some sources suggest he never wanted the throne and accepted it out of duty. He kept many of Augustus's policies, focusing on maintaining order in the provinces and keeping the army loyal. Tiberius was strict with finances, leaving a surplus in the treasury. Early in his reign, he showed respect for the Senate, continuing the show of a shared government.

Growing Suspicion

Over time, Tiberius became more distant. He relied heavily on his advisor **Sejanus**, the leader of the Praetorian Guard, who gained significant influence. Many senators feared Sejanus's power. Conspiracies and rumors flourished, leading Tiberius to crack down on real or imagined plots. Treason trials became common, and informers thrived by accusing wealthy people of disloyalty. Tiberius moved to the island of **Capri** in AD 26, rarely visiting Rome. From Capri, he governed through letters and messengers, further damaging his relations with the Senate.

Eventually, Tiberius turned against Sejanus, suspecting him of aiming for the throne. Sejanus was arrested and executed in AD 31, along with many of his supporters. The final years of Tiberius's rule were marked by fear and mistrust. When he died in AD 37, many Romans were relieved. Nevertheless, Tiberius had kept the empire stable, ensuring no major revolts or economic crises.

Caligula (AD 37–41)

A Sudden Shift

Tiberius's successor was **Gaius Julius Caesar Germanicus**, nicknamed **Caligula** (meaning "little soldier's boot," from his childhood among the troops). Initially, the people rejoiced. Caligula was the son of the beloved general Germanicus, and they hoped for a return to the happy days of Augustus. Indeed, Caligula began by granting bonuses to soldiers, hosting lavish games, and pardoning many prisoners. But within months, he fell seriously ill. After recovering, his behavior changed drastically, at least according to many ancient sources.

Tales of Excess and Madness

Caligula's short reign became infamous for cruelty and extravagance. Stories claim he spent huge sums on parties, forced wealthy citizens to give him money, and demanded to be treated like a living god. Some accounts even say he wanted to make his horse, Incitatus, a consul—though this might be exaggerated gossip.

He argued with the Senate, executed people without proper trials, and humiliated leading families. While some details may be exaggerated by hostile writers, it is clear Caligula's rule frightened and angered Rome's elite. In AD 41, members of the Praetorian Guard conspired against him. They attacked and killed Caligula in a palace corridor, putting an end to his chaotic reign.

Claudius (AD 41–54)

The Unexpected Emperor

After Caligula's assassination, the conspirators did not have a clear successor. In the confusion, the Praetorian Guard found **Claudius**, Caligula's uncle, hiding behind a curtain in the palace. They proclaimed him emperor. Claudius, seen by some as clumsy and timid, had been largely ignored by his family. Yet he proved a surprisingly capable ruler.

Administrative Reforms and Conquests

Claudius improved the empire's administration, relying on talented freedmen as secretaries for correspondence and finance. He also focused on public works—building roads, aqueducts, and new harbor facilities at Ostia. One of his most notable achievements was the **invasion of Britain** in AD 43. Rome had briefly visited Britain under Julius Caesar, but Claudius made it a province. Generals under Claudius secured a foothold in southeast Britain, bringing parts of the island into the empire.

Claudius tried to respect the Senate, but he also used equestrians and freedmen to manage government tasks more efficiently. Some senators resented this, feeling sidelined by the emperor's "non-noble" assistants. Claudius's personal life was stormy. He married several times, and his last wife, **Agrippina the Younger**, was ambitious and determined to secure the throne for her son, **Nero**. Claudius died in AD 54, possibly poisoned by Agrippina. Despite political intrigues, he left the empire more extensive and better organized than before.

Nero (AD 54–68)

Popular Beginnings

When Claudius died, **Nero**—age 16 or 17—became emperor. Early in his reign, he was guided by his mother Agrippina, his tutor the philosopher **Seneca**, and the praetorian prefect **Burrus**. They helped him govern wisely at first, passing moderate laws and cutting taxes. Nero sponsored games, theater, and music competitions, winning favor among common people. He wanted to be known for his artistic talents—especially singing and playing the lyre.

Conflicts and Downfall

As Nero grew older, he clashed with those who tried to control him. He pushed his mother aside and eventually had her killed in AD 59 to remove her influence. Seneca and Burrus lost their power; Burrus died, and Seneca retired. Without their guidance, Nero drifted into extravagance. He taxed the provinces harshly to fund his lavish projects.

In AD 64, a massive fire ravaged Rome. Some blamed Nero, claiming he wanted to rebuild the city to his own design, or that he was seen "fiddling" (playing music) during the blaze. Whether true or not,

Nero rebuilt parts of Rome, constructing a grand palace called the **Domus Aurea** (Golden House). Seeking scapegoats for the fire, he accused **Christians**, then a small, misunderstood group, of starting it. Many were executed, marking the empire's first major persecution of Christians.

A series of revolts broke out, including one led by the governor **Vindex** in Gaul. The Senate turned against Nero, declaring him an enemy of the state. Facing betrayal by the army and the Senate, Nero fled Rome. Unable to find support, he took his own life in AD 68. His death ended the Julio-Claudian line. Rome now faced a dangerous power vacuum.

The Year of the Four Emperors (AD 68–69)

After Nero's death, no direct heir from Augustus's family remained. Four different men claimed the throne in quick succession:

1. **Galba**: A governor in Spain who marched to Rome, supported by the Senate. But he was unpopular with the army due to strict discipline and stingy payments.
2. **Otho**: Once a friend of Nero, he staged a coup and overthrew Galba. He reigned for a few months until the legions in Germany declared **Vitellius** emperor.
3. **Vitellius**: Defeated Otho's forces. Then Vitellius himself faced revolt from the eastern legions.
4. **Vespasian**: A successful general who had been fighting the Jewish revolt in Judea. His troops proclaimed him emperor, and he marched on Rome. Vitellius was killed, and Vespasian secured power by late AD 69.

These civil wars caused chaos, as different armies fought for their chosen emperors. However, once **Vespasian** won, stability began to return, ushering in the **Flavian dynasty**.

The Flavian Dynasty (AD 69–96)

Vespasian (AD 69–79)

Titus Flavius Vespasianus, known simply as **Vespasian**, came from a relatively modest background in the Italian countryside. He was a capable soldier, serving under Claudius in Britain and later entrusted by Nero with suppressing the Jewish revolt in Judea. After seizing power in AD 69, Vespasian worked to stabilize finances, restore discipline in the army, and rebuild Rome's damaged infrastructure.

He was known for his down-to-earth manner and sense of humor. To raise funds, he taxed many activities, even imposing a tax on public urinals (famously joked about as "money does not stink"). Vespasian also began constructing the **Flavian Amphitheater**, later called the **Colosseum**, on the site of Nero's demolished palace gardens. This grand arena symbolized a return to public pleasure venues and a break with Nero's self-indulgence.

Titus (AD 79–81)

Vespasian's elder son, **Titus**, succeeded him peacefully. Titus had already gained fame as a military commander, completing the conquest of Jerusalem in AD 70. As emperor, he faced two disasters:

1. **Eruption of Mount Vesuvius (AD 79):** This volcano erupted near Naples, destroying **Pompeii** and **Herculaneum**. Titus provided aid to the survivors, earning praise for his swift response.
2. **A Major Fire in Rome (AD 80):** He again offered relief to the homeless.

Titus also dedicated the Colosseum, holding 100 days of games and gladiatorial contests. Known for his generosity and kindness, Titus died young in AD 81, possibly from natural causes.

Domitian (AD 81–96)

Domitian, Titus's younger brother, succeeded him. Domitian aimed to restore the monarchy's grandeur, insisting on being addressed as "Lord and God" (*Dominus et Deus*). He fought wars along the Danube and in Britain, seeking military glory. At home, he improved Rome's economy and revalued coinage, but he was autocratic, clashing with the Senate and using treason trials to root out opponents.

Domitian built impressive structures, such as the **Arch of Titus** to honor his brother's victories. However, his fear of conspiracies led to increasing executions. Eventually, a plot involving palace officials and possibly his wife succeeded in assassinating Domitian in AD 96. The Senate, which disliked him, quickly condemned his memory. Despite this, Domitian had maintained order and built up frontier defenses. His death ended the Flavian dynasty.

Roman Society Under the Early Emperors

Despite the dramas at the top, life for most Romans continued day by day. The empire's administrative system, shaped by Augustus, largely remained in place. Provincial governors collected taxes, legionaries patrolled the frontiers, and trade networks linked distant regions. During stable reigns (such as Claudius's or Vespasian's), people enjoyed public works, entertainment, and relative peace, at least in the empire's core areas.

When an emperor acted cruelly—like Caligula or Nero—the elite in Rome suffered the most, facing purges and confiscations. The provinces were sometimes less affected, as local authorities still managed routine affairs. Periodic wars or revolts (like the Jewish revolt) caused regional devastation, but they did not usually disrupt the empire as a whole unless civil war erupted.

Notable Events and Projects

1. **Colosseum Construction** under Vespasian and Titus: This grand amphitheater became a symbol of Roman engineering and public entertainment.
2. **Expansion in Britain**: Claudius's conquest and subsequent campaigns extended Roman influence, though full control of the island was never achieved.
3. **Imperial Cult Growth**: Emperors were honored—sometimes worshiped—after their deaths. Temples to deceased emperors were built, uniting the empire under shared rituals.
4. **Vesuvius Eruption (AD 79)**: A major natural disaster, leaving behind archaeological treasures at Pompeii and Herculaneum for modern study.
5. **Arch of Titus**: Constructed by Domitian to celebrate Titus's capture of Jerusalem. It depicted the spoils of the Jewish Temple, signifying Roman victory.

Transition to the Next Era

By AD 96, Rome had survived five emperors from the Julio-Claudian line (including the short reign of Caligula) and three Flavians. The Senate, weary of paranoia and violence, turned to an older, respected senator named **Nerva**, who became emperor by Senate choice. With Nerva's accession, the Roman Empire moved toward a more stable and celebrated period—an era that would see five consecutive rulers praised for their wisdom and good governance.

CHAPTER 14

ROME'S GOLDEN AGE AND THE FIVE GOOD EMPERORS

A Time of Stability

In the late 1st and early 2nd centuries AD, the Roman Empire reached a level of stability and prosperity seldom seen before or since. Historians often call the period from **Nerva's** accession in AD 96 to the death of **Marcus Aurelius** in AD 180 the age of the **Five Good Emperors**. These rulers—**Nerva**, **Trajan**, **Hadrian**, **Antoninus Pius**, and **Marcus Aurelius**—were known for their moderate governance, fair treatment of provinces, and relative lack of destructive ambition.

This "golden age" did not mean everything was perfect. Rome still fought wars and faced economic challenges. But by choosing or adopting worthy successors (rather than relying on direct family lines), these emperors avoided many of the dynastic struggles that had plagued earlier reigns. As a result, the Senate, equestrians, and common people generally supported them, maintaining a sense of unity across the empire.

Nerva (AD 96–98)

The Elder Statesman

After Domitian's assassination, the Senate swiftly chose **Marcus Cocceius Nerva**, a respected older senator with a calm reputation. Though advanced in age, Nerva promised to restore freedoms lost under Domitian and to rule with the Senate's advice. He also ended treason trials and recalled exiles.

However, Nerva lacked strong military backing. The Praetorian Guard, still bitter over Domitian's death, demanded punishments for Domitian's killers. Nerva had little choice but to comply, signifying that the real power was still in the hands of the army. Realizing he needed a capable heir who could control the legions, Nerva adopted **Trajan**, a popular general stationed on the Rhine frontier. This move secured the empire's loyalty to Nerva. When Nerva died peacefully in AD 98, the empire transitioned smoothly to Trajan.

Trajan (AD 98–117)

Rome's Greatest Extent

Marcus Ulpius Traianus, known as **Trajan**, was born in Italica (in modern Spain), making him the first emperor from a province rather than Italy itself. He was already famous for his military skill and fair leadership. As emperor, Trajan embarked on successful conquests that pushed Rome's boundaries to their furthest point:

1. **Dacian Wars (AD 101–102, 105–106)**: Trajan conquered **Dacia** (roughly modern Romania), a rich region of gold mines. He commemorated his victory with **Trajan's Column**, a monumental relief telling the story of the campaigns.
2. **Parthian Campaign (AD 113–117)**: Trajan invaded Mesopotamia, taking the important cities of **Arsacid** territory (near the Parthian kingdom). He reached the Persian Gulf, making the empire larger than ever before.

These expansions brought tremendous wealth in the form of gold, land, and trade routes. However, holding Mesopotamia proved difficult. By the end of Trajan's life, rebellions broke out, and his Eastern gains seemed precarious. Still, his conquests made him legendary in Roman eyes, and the Senate honored him with the title **Optimus Princeps** ("Best Ruler").

Public Works and Reforms

Trajan was also admired for his care of the provinces. He built roads, improved harbors, and founded new cities. In Italy, he created the **alimenta** program, offering loans to farmers at low interest, with the interest used to support orphans and poor children. His grand building projects in Rome included **Trajan's Forum** and **Trajan's Market**, an early version of a multi-level shopping complex.

Unlike some earlier emperors, Trajan listened to the Senate, often writing them respectful letters about military and administrative issues. He died in AD 117 while returning from his Parthian campaign. Childless, he named his cousin **Hadrian** as successor.

Hadrian (AD 117–138)

Securing the Frontiers

Publius Aelius Hadrianus, known as **Hadrian**, was also from a Spanish family. He reversed some of Trajan's expansions, pulling back from Mesopotamia because it was too costly to maintain. Instead, Hadrian aimed to strengthen existing borders:

- **Hadrian's Wall (in Britain):** Marking the northern limit of Roman control in Britain, this stone-and-turf fortification stretched about 73 miles. It included forts and watchtowers to keep out northern tribes (the Picts or Caledonians).
- **Fortified Frontiers:** Across the Rhine and Danube, Hadrian built or improved **limes** (border defenses), ensuring better security for the provinces.

Traveling Emperor

Hadrian spent much of his reign traveling across the empire—visiting provinces from Britain to Syria, from Africa to Asia

Minor. He inspected troops, resolved local disputes, and initiated building projects. In Greece, he admired Athens, building monumental structures and promoting Greek art and learning. Hadrian's passion for Greek culture led him to style himself as a philhellene (lover of Greek ways).

His personal life included a deep friendship with a young Greek named **Antinous**, whose early death caused the emperor great grief. Hadrian founded cities and built monuments in Antinous's honor, a move that raised eyebrows but also showcased the emperor's absolute power to shape culture and religion.

Internal Reforms

Hadrian codified Roman law, encouraging jurists to create a more consistent legal framework. He reorganized the civil service, establishing permanent offices with clearly defined powers. In Rome, he built the famous **Pantheon** we know today, replacing an older structure. The Pantheon's dome—still the largest unreinforced concrete dome—testifies to Rome's advanced engineering.

Hadrian's last years were overshadowed by a Jewish revolt in Judea (132–135 AD), triggered by his plan to build a Roman colony on Jerusalem's ruins. The revolt was crushed brutally, scattering the Jewish population. When Hadrian died in AD 138, he left behind a more defensible empire and a strong administrative system.

Antoninus Pius (AD 138–161)

Peace and Prosperity

Hadrian adopted **Antoninus Pius**, instructing him to adopt **Marcus Aurelius** and a young Lucius Verus as successors. **Titus Aelius Hadrianus Antoninus**, called **Antoninus Pius**, had a calm, balanced approach to ruling. Under him, Rome experienced a largely peaceful time, with no major wars. Antoninus Pius believed in consolidating gains rather than expanding. His reign was marked by diplomatic efforts, stable finances, and public works.

Antoninus Pius was often praised for his piety, fairness, and the good relations he kept with the Senate. He oversaw the finishing touches on many building projects started by Hadrian, including the final work on the **Temple of the Deified Hadrian**. He also pushed Roman frontiers slightly in Britain, building the short-lived **Antonine Wall** north of Hadrian's Wall, though it was soon abandoned for the more secure older line.

Legal Improvements

Antoninus Pius continued reforms in Roman law, working closely with top jurists. He emphasized justice for provincial citizens, punishing corrupt governors. The empire's economy generally thrived, benefiting from stable leadership and robust trade. When Antoninus Pius died in AD 161, after 23 years of relative peace, people across the empire mourned him.

Marcus Aurelius and Lucius Verus

Joint Rule (AD 161-169)

When Antoninus Pius died, **Marcus Aurelius** and **Lucius Verus** became joint emperors—an unusual arrangement in Rome. Marcus Aurelius was Antoninus's adopted son, widely admired for his intellect and devotion to Stoic philosophy. Lucius Verus was also adopted by Antoninus, though he was known more for enjoying luxuries and games.

This dual rule was tested immediately by wars:

1. **War with Parthia (AD 161-166):** Lucius Verus led campaigns in the East, though generals under him did much of the fighting. They succeeded, but returning troops brought a plague back to Rome, causing high mortality across the empire.
2. **Northern Frontiers:** Germanic and other tribes tested the Danube defenses. Marcus Aurelius would spend much of his reign dealing with these threats.

Marcus Aurelius: The Philosopher-Emperor

When Lucius Verus died in AD 169 (possibly from the plague), Marcus Aurelius became sole emperor. Known for his work **Meditations**, written in Greek, he reflected on duty, virtue, and self-control, embodying Stoic ideals. Yet his reign was far from peaceful. He had to lead multiple campaigns against Marcomanni, Quadi, and other tribes pressing into Roman territory along the Danube.

Despite these wars, Marcus Aurelius showed compassion for the empire's people. He sold palace valuables to fund war costs, and he tried to ensure fair justice. However, continuous fighting strained Rome's resources. The plague reduced the population and army manpower. Marcus Aurelius spent years on military campaigns, rarely enjoying life in Rome. He died in AD 180 during a campaign on the Danube frontier.

End of the Golden Age

Commodus's Succession

Unlike previous Good Emperors who adopted capable successors, Marcus Aurelius broke the pattern by leaving the throne to his biological son, **Commodus**. This marked a return to hereditary rule, which would prove problematic. Commodus was not well-suited for the role. Though we will discuss him more in Chapter 15, many historians see his reign (AD 180–192) as the end of Rome's golden age.

Achievements and Legacy

The "Five Good Emperors" built an era of:

- **Steady Governance:** Fewer purges or treason trials, more cooperation with the Senate.
- **Strong Defense but Limited Expansion:** Borders were fortified (e.g., Hadrian's Wall), with only Trajan pushing for major conquests.

- **Cultural Flourishing:** Law, architecture, and arts thrived, blending local customs with Roman rule. Large building projects like Trajan's Forum, Hadrian's Pantheon, and improvements under Antoninus Pius showed the empire's wealth.
- **Economic Vitality:** Trade networks linked provinces, while stable currencies and fair administration encouraged growth.
- **Philosophical Outlook:** Marcus Aurelius embodied a ruler who sought wisdom and virtue in times of crisis.

Yet even the greatest stability could not prevent future challenges. The empire's vastness, external pressures, and internal politics would bring new trials after AD 180. Still, many Romans of later times looked back on the era of Nerva to Marcus Aurelius as the high point of imperial civilization.

Society and Culture Under the Good Emperors

During this golden period:

1. **Cities Prospered**: Roman towns from Africa to Britain built forums, theaters, and temples, supported by imperial and local elites.
2. **Legal Unity**: Edicts and rulings from the emperors, along with famous jurists (e.g., Salvius Julianus, Papinian), clarified Roman law, influencing future civilizations.
3. **Art and Architecture**: The empire saw advanced engineering, from bridging major rivers to constructing elaborate aqueducts. Large-scale statues and relief sculptures (e.g., the Column of Marcus Aurelius) celebrated imperial victories.
4. **Religious Diversity**: Traditional gods, emperor worship, mystery cults (like Mithraism), Judaism, and the growing Christian movement all coexisted, sometimes with tensions. Persecutions flared up now and then, but not to the scale seen under emperors like Nero or Domitian (except in certain local cases).

5. **Philosophical Influence**: Stoicism guided many elite Romans, promoting duty, self-discipline, and moral uprightness. Marcus Aurelius's *Meditations* remains a famous testament to this mindset.

Conclusion of the Golden Age

With Marcus Aurelius's death in AD 180, the "Five Good Emperors" tradition ended. While Commodus took over, he lacked his father's dedication and wisdom, plunging Rome into a less stable era. Still, the achievements of Nerva, Trajan, Hadrian, Antoninus Pius, and Marcus Aurelius left a deep mark on Roman history, often remembered as the pinnacle of enlightened rule.

CHAPTER 15

EVERYDAY LIFE IN IMPERIAL ROME

Stepping into Daily Life

So far, we have talked about the **emperors**, the **wars**, and the **major events** of Rome's history. But what was life like for the people who lived in the empire day by day? In this chapter, we will **step away from battles and politics** to look at **everyday life in Imperial Rome**. This period roughly spans the first few centuries AD, especially the era after Augustus established the Principate.

During this time, Rome was a vast empire stretching across Europe, North Africa, and parts of Asia. The population of the city of Rome itself may have reached **one million** or more. People of many backgrounds—rich and poor, free and enslaved, Roman-born or from faraway provinces—shared the bustling streets, markets, and public squares. Although differences in wealth and social status were huge, certain patterns of daily life ran through all classes.

Social Classes and the Family

Patricians, Equestrians, Plebeians

By the time of the empire, the old division between **patricians** (the original noble families) and **plebeians** (the commoners) remained, but it was no longer the only measure of status. Wealth and political connections mattered more than ancient family background. Another important class was the **equestrians** (or "knights"), people with enough money to qualify for certain privileges but who were not senators. Many equestrians ran businesses, served as imperial administrators, or dealt in trade.

At the top of society stood the **senatorial class**, traditionally from the richest families, often holding offices in the Senate. Below them came the equestrians, followed by wealthy plebeians. Most inhabitants of Rome, however, were ordinary folk: artisans, shopkeepers, laborers, or unemployed citizens living off the imperial grain dole. And at the bottom were slaves—men, women, and children owned by others.

The Roman Family (Paterfamilias)

In theory, the **paterfamilias** (the oldest male) held power over the family. He could arrange marriages, control finances, and even decide life or death for newborn babies in old times. However, by the imperial period, these extreme powers were rarely used. Still, the father or grandfather was highly respected, and his authority shaped family decisions.

Marriage often had an element of business or social alliances, especially among the elite. A father might arrange for a daughter to marry a man who would benefit the family's political or economic standing. Love was not always the main factor, but many couples grew close over time. Women had more freedom than in earlier ages, managing household affairs and sometimes running their own businesses. Elite women could own property and influence social events, though they could not hold official political roles.

Children were expected to obey their elders. Boys from wealthy families had tutors or went to private schools to learn reading, writing, arithmetic, and sometimes Greek language. Girls might also learn basic literacy, along with skills like spinning, weaving, and managing servants.

Slaves and Freedmen

Slavery in Daily Life

Slavery was a huge part of Roman society. Enslaved people came from conquered territories, were born into slave families, or sold themselves into slavery if they were deeply in debt. Slaves could be found **everywhere**: working in households, on farms, in mines, and even managing shops for their masters. In rich homes, dozens or even hundreds of slaves might serve as cooks, cleaners, tutors, or personal attendants.

Slaves had no legal rights. They could not marry legally, although many formed family-like relationships known as **contubernium**. Their masters had the power to punish or sell them, though laws over time tried to protect slaves from extreme cruelty. Some slaves—especially those with special skills or trust—could earn money on the side (their **peculium**) and hope to buy their freedom.

Becoming a Freedman

If a master freed a slave, that person became a **freedman** (or freedwoman). Freedmen had limited citizenship: they could own property, marry, and start a business, but they could not hold high political office. Many freedmen remained tied to their former masters as **clients**, offering loyalty or services. A few became very wealthy—especially those who worked as imperial administrators or managed large enterprises—and they sometimes helped shape Roman life in significant ways.

The children of freedmen, born after their parents gained freedom, usually had **full Roman citizenship**. Thus, a family could rise from slavery to citizen status within a generation. This path to integration was one reason Roman society, despite its cruelty in allowing slavery, remained somewhat flexible about new influences and talents.

Housing: Rich Villas and Crowded Tenements

Domus (City Houses for the Wealthy)

Wealthy Romans lived in **domus**, single-family houses with multiple rooms centered around an **atrium** (an open courtyard) and a **peristyle** (a garden surrounded by columns). The atrium had a hole in the roof and a basin on the floor to collect rainwater. Frescoes and mosaics decorated walls and floors. Bedrooms (cubicula), dining rooms (triclinia), kitchens, and offices (tablinum) connected to these central areas.

Some elite homes were quite large, especially in neighborhoods on the Palatine Hill or other upscale districts. They might feature sculptures, fountains, and elaborate wall paintings. Wealthy owners hosted banquets in their triclinia, impressing guests with fine tableware and exotic foods. However, due to the city's density, many aristocrats also owned villas in the countryside or by the sea, where they could escape Rome's noise and heat.

Insulae (Apartment Buildings for Commoners)

The majority of city dwellers lived in **insulae**—multi-story apartment buildings constructed of brick and wood. Ground floors might house shops or taverns, while families crowded into upper floors with minimal space. Rents varied; the higher the floor, the cheaper (and often more dangerous) the apartment. Fires were a constant risk, since cooking was done on small braziers, and buildings were not always stable.

In better insulae, tenants might have a shared latrine and access to fresh water from aqueduct-fed fountains in the street. Poorer insulae lacked basic amenities. Garbage disposal was erratic, leading to dirty, smelly conditions. Despite these hardships, insula living offered community life: neighbors interacted in stairwells, courtyards, and local shops. Street vendors sold hot bread or cooked pulses, and children played games in the alleys.

A Typical Day in the City

Morning Activities

Most free Romans woke up early. If they were wealthy, slaves helped them dress. Men might wear a **tunic** indoors and a **toga** for public business or formal occasions. Women wore **stolas** (long dresses) and palla shawls. The father might hold a quick **salutatio**, greeting clients who visited each morning for advice, money, or political requests. Afterward, he could head to the Forum for business, law courts, or Senate meetings.

Ordinary workers—artisans, shopkeepers, laborers—opened their shops or joined building crews at dawn, taking advantage of cooler morning hours. Markets bustled with fishmongers, produce sellers, and butchers setting up stalls. Bakers delivered fresh bread from their ovens. Slaves ran errands for their masters, buying food or delivering messages.

Midday Pause

Around midday, many Romans took a break. Shops closed briefly in the afternoon. Some people might have a **light lunch** (often bread, cheese, fruits) or a short rest. Wealthy individuals might retire to the baths early or catch up on reading or leisure. However, lower-class citizens often kept working if they needed the income. Because of Rome's hot climate, especially in summer, pausing at midday offered relief from the sun.

Late Afternoon and Evening

In the later afternoon, many citizens went to the **public baths** (thermae) for exercise, bathing, and socializing (we will explore this more in Part 2). Afterward, families gathered for the main meal of the day, the **cena**. Patrons and clients might dine together, discussing politics and gossip. Street life in many districts stayed lively until dark, with taverns, snack stalls, and communal gatherings in the street.

Nighttime was dimly lit, as oil lamps and torches were the main sources of light. Danger from criminals sometimes increased on dark streets. City authorities tried to maintain order, but the late hours could be rowdy. People often went to bed early, knowing they would rise with the dawn.

Varied Lives Across the Empire

While we focus on Rome, remember that millions of people lived in other cities—like Carthage, Alexandria, Antioch, and Ephesus—or in rural villages throughout the provinces. Daily life varied with local customs and climates. But the Romans shared certain core elements: the Latin language (especially in the West), Roman laws, and the presence of baths, forums, and temples. Greek language and culture remained very influential in the Eastern provinces, where many people were bilingual.

Roman roads connected these regions, carrying travelers, merchants, and official couriers. Large ships transported grain from Egypt and Africa to feed Rome's hungry population. In the countryside, farmers grew wheat, olives, and grapes on estates, using slaves or tenant farmers. Soldiers on frontier postings had their own routines, living in forts and building small towns around them.

Food and Dining Customs

Common Foods

Grain was the mainstay of the Roman diet, typically made into **bread** or **porridge**. Wealthy households enjoyed a variety of meats (pork, poultry, and sometimes beef), fish, and vegetables. **Olive oil** and **wine** were staples across all classes. Vegetables like **cabbage**, **lettuce**, **garlic**, and **leeks** were common, along with fruits such as **figs**, **apples**, **grapes**, and **dates**. Poorer citizens often relied on simple meals—bread with cheese, beans, or porridge. Meat could be a luxury.

The empire's trade routes brought **spices** and **sauces** from faraway regions. A famous sauce was **garum**, a fish sauce used to flavor many dishes. Wealthy banquets included exotic fare—like flamingo, ostrich, or dormice stuffed with nuts. However, such treats were expensive and aimed at showing off the host's wealth.

The Roman Cena (Main Meal)

Romans generally ate three meals a day:

1. **Ientaculum** (breakfast): Light—bread, olives, possibly leftovers.
2. **Prandium** (lunch): Also light—cold meats, bread, fruits.
3. **Cena** (dinner): The main and longest meal. Wealthy people reclined on couches around a **triclinium** (dining table with three sides). Slaves served multiple courses, from appetizers (eggs, salads) to main dishes of fish or meat, finishing with fruits or sweets. **Wine mixed with water** accompanied the meal.

Banquets could last hours, featuring entertainment—dancers, musicians, or poetry readings. Guests discussed politics, philosophy, or local gossip. Poorer Romans, on the other hand, often ate a simple one-pot meal at the end of the day, perhaps in a small insula room or a tavern.

Public Entertainment and Leisure

The Baths (Thermae)

One of the most characteristic social hubs was the **public baths**. Contrary to modern ideas, these baths were not just for washing; they were places to exercise, relax, and meet friends. A typical large bath complex might include:

- **Palaestra** (exercise yard) for wrestling or ball games.
- **Apodyterium** (changing room).
- **Caldarium** (hot room) for soaking in steamy water.
- **Tepidarium** (warm room).
- **Frigidarium** (cold plunge pool).

Men and women usually bathed separately or at different times (though some private or smaller baths might allow mixed bathing). The bath complexes often had gardens, libraries, and snack bars. Entrance fees were low, making them accessible to most free citizens. Bathing was an afternoon ritual for many—an opportunity to unwind and socialize.

Chariot Races (Circus Maximus)

Racing teams, each identified by a color (Reds, Greens, Blues, Whites), attracted passionate fans. The **Circus Maximus** in Rome could hold hundreds of thousands of spectators. Charioteers, sometimes slaves or freedmen, became celebrities if they won enough races. The crowd cheered, bet on outcomes, and supported their favorite team with intense loyalty. Races were fast and dangerous—accidents known as "shipwrecks" occurred when chariots collided or overturned.

Gladiatorial Games (Amphitheaters)

Gladiators fought in **amphitheaters**, the most famous being the **Colosseum** (Flavian Amphitheater). These fighters were trained in special schools. Some were prisoners of war, slaves, or volunteers seeking fame. Contests might pit one gladiator style against another (e.g., a heavily armored murmillo vs. a nimble retiarius armed with a net and trident). The crowd roared with excitement. If a gladiator was wounded, the sponsor of the games could decide his fate by listening to the spectators. Not all fights ended in death, but many did.

Beyond gladiators, there were also **animal hunts** (venationes), where hunters faced wild beasts like lions or bears brought from Africa or Asia. These spectacles were expensive to stage, but emperors and wealthy patrons used them to win public favor. For common people, the games were thrilling entertainment, though they could be brutal.

Religious Practices and Festivals

Roman Gods and Household Worship

Romans worshiped many gods, each with specific roles—**Jupiter** as king of the gods, **Juno** protecting marriage, **Minerva** for wisdom, **Mars** for war, and so on. People prayed and offered sacrifices at **temples** or household altars. In homes, families kept small statues of **Lares** and **Penates** (household gods), making daily offerings of food or incense.

Religion in Rome was about **ritual correctness**. Priests (pontifices) or specialized colleges performed official ceremonies, examining animal entrails or interpreting omens from birds. The emperor served as **Pontifex Maximus**, overseeing state religion. Foreign gods or cults, like the Egyptian goddess **Isis**, found acceptance in Rome, too. Some, like the **Mithras** cult (popular among soldiers), held secret ceremonies in underground chambers.

Public Festivals

Festivals punctuated the Roman calendar, celebrating gods, harvest times, or historical events. During major festivals, business paused, and families attended processions, feasts, and public games. Examples include:

- **Saturnalia (December)**: A time of merrymaking, gift-giving, and role reversals, when masters served slaves at meals in a spirit of fun.
- **Lupercalia (February)**: A fertility festival where priests ran around the Palatine, striking bystanders lightly with goat-skin thongs to bring good luck.
- **Secular Games**: Held occasionally to mark new eras or important anniversaries, featuring sporting events and sacrifices.

The city bustled with color, music, and street vendors during these holidays. For many Romans, these festivals brought joy and a sense of shared identity.

Community and Neighborhood Life

The Forum and Other Public Spaces

In Rome, the **Forum** was the heart of public life, surrounded by temples, basilicas (public halls), and shops. People came to hear political speeches, watch trials, or do business deals. Over time, emperors built additional forums—like the **Forum of Trajan**—to handle the crowds and reflect their power. Citizens could also gather in open-air markets, squares near large public buildings, and porticoes that offered shelter from rain or sun.

Neighborhoods had their own local shrines and meeting spots. Street vendors called out, selling food or goods. Children played ball games, knucklebones, or ran races in open areas. Fire brigades and watchmen (the vigiles) patrolled at night to prevent fires or crime, though success varied. The city was full of noise—from artisans hammering metal to animals being herded through narrow streets.

Taverns and Social Clubs

For socializing, people often visited **taverns** (tabernae) or **popinae**, which served simple meals and wine. Travelers stayed at inns, though many Romans preferred lodging with friends or clients. Another aspect of social life was belonging to **collegia** (guilds or clubs) for workers in the same trade or for worshipers of a particular deity. These clubs offered fellowship, held banquets, and sometimes provided funeral insurance. They helped form small communities in the vastness of Rome.

The Challenges of City Life

Roman cities could be exciting but also **dangerous**:

- **Fire** threatened insulae often.
- **Crime** ranged from pickpocketing to nighttime robberies.
- **Health Issues** included poor sanitation, especially in crowded slums. Sewers like the Cloaca Maxima helped, but not everyone had access to good drainage.
- **Overpopulation** meant many were jobless, depending on the grain dole for basic food.
- **Pollution** from open fires and the lack of rubbish disposal gave the city a distinctive smell.

However, to offset these hardships, the emperors offered **"bread and circuses"**—cheap grain and free entertainment—to keep the masses content. Rich philanthropists might fund public projects, feeling social or political pressure to display generosity.

Looking Back at Daily Life

We have now explored how Romans lived from day to day: their homes, meals, baths, entertainments, and festivals. Life varied wildly depending on one's **wealth** and **status**. Yet certain elements—like the love of gatherings, the importance of religion, and the reliance on slaves—ran through the entire empire.

In the next chapter, **Chapter 16: Challenges and the Crisis of the Third Century**, we will return to the broader political scene. As we move into the 3rd century AD, the Roman Empire faces **new pressures**: foreign invasions, economic troubles, and a series of short-lived emperors often chosen by the army. This crisis period will severely test the social fabric we have just seen, ushering in reforms that change the face of Rome forever.

CHAPTER 16

CHALLENGES AND THE CRISIS OF THE THIRD CENTURY

A Turbulent Century Begins

The 2nd century AD ended on a high note with the stable rule of the "Five Good Emperors," but cracks were forming. When **Marcus Aurelius** died in AD 180, his son **Commodus** became emperor, signaling a shift away from the era of wise, adopted successors. Over the next decades, problems multiplied: **barbarian invasions**, **plague**, **economic troubles**, and internal power struggles. By the mid-3rd century, the empire plunged into a prolonged crisis known as the **Crisis of the Third Century**.

This crisis shook Rome to its core. In a span of roughly 50 years (AD 235–284), numerous emperors and usurpers vied for power, the frontiers crumbled in places, and the economy nearly collapsed. Yet from this turmoil came major reforms that laid foundations for a more centralized and autocratic system. In Part 1 of Chapter 16, we look at the earlier part of the 3rd century—how instability began, how outside threats grew, and how soldier-emperors rose to power. In Part 2, we will see how the empire faced near-breakdown and the steps taken by leaders like **Aurelian** and **Diocletian** to save it.

Commodus (AD 180–192)

The End of the Golden Era

Commodus, the son of Marcus Aurelius, was a stark contrast to his father. He preferred **gladiatorial games** and personal pleasures, neglecting state affairs. Ancient writers describe him as cruel, vain, and extravagant. He fought in the arena as if he were a gladiator, shocking the Senate. He also claimed divine status, renaming Rome **Colonia Lucia Annia Commodiana** at one point.

Despite these extremes, Commodus did keep peace on some frontiers, thanks to the army's strength. But corruption and mismanagement grew at home. By AD 192, his behavior outraged senators, the Praetorian Guard, and even his closest allies. A conspiracy ended with Commodus's assassination. With no heir, Rome again faced a power vacuum.

The Severan Dynasty (AD 193–235)

After Commodus, civil war erupted. Several contenders rose:

- **Pertinax**, a respected senator, was briefly emperor but was killed by the Praetorian Guard after refusing to pay them large sums.
- The Guard then "auctioned" the empire to **Didius Julianus**, who offered the highest bribe. But provincial legions refused to accept this humiliating process.
- Three generals—**Septimius Severus**, **Pescennius Niger**, and **Clodius Albinus**—competed. By AD 197, **Septimius Severus** emerged victorious.

Septimius Severus (AD 193–211)

Severus, born in Leptis Magna (North Africa), built power on the army's loyalty. He disbanded the Praetorian Guard that killed Pertinax, replacing them with his own men. Severus fought campaigns in the East and against barbarians along the Danube. He also reformed the administration, favoring soldiers and raising their pay. "Enrich the soldiers, and scorn the rest," one quote suggests was his guiding policy.

At home, he expanded the role of jurists and created new legal precedents. His rule was harsh but effective in keeping control. Before he died in AD 211, he advised his sons, **Caracalla** and **Geta**, to remain unified and keep the army well rewarded.

Caracalla (AD 211–217)

Caracalla quickly murdered his brother Geta and ruled alone. He is famous for the **Edict of Caracalla** (AD 212), granting **Roman citizenship** to nearly all free inhabitants of the empire. While this might seem generous, it also increased tax revenue by expanding the pool of those who owed certain taxes. Caracalla built the massive **Baths of Caracalla** in Rome, showcasing imperial grandeur. However, he led expensive military campaigns and faced plots. He was assassinated in AD 217 by his own troops.

Later Severans

- **Macrinus** (AD 217–218), Caracalla's Praetorian prefect, took power briefly but lost support of the legions.
- **Elagabalus** (AD 218–222), a young and eccentric emperor from the Severan family, tried imposing the worship of the sun god El-Gabal. His bizarre behavior, including strange religious rites, led to his assassination.
- **Severus Alexander** (AD 222–235) then ruled, guided by his mother Julia Mamaea. He tried moderate policies, but growing external threats demanded stronger military leadership. In AD 235, troops near the Rhine frontier revolted, killing him. This event marked the start of the worst crisis in Rome's history so far.

The Rise of Soldier-Emperors

Barbarian Pressure

By the mid-3rd century, several **Germanic tribes** (Alamanni, Goths, Franks) and **Sarmatians** pressed on the Rhine-Danube frontiers. In the East, the **Sassanid Empire** replaced the Parthians, led by vigorous kings like **Shapur I**. They invaded Roman territories in Mesopotamia and captured the emperor **Valerian** in AD 260—a humiliating moment that showed how vulnerable Rome had become.

Frontier legions grew restless, proclaiming their successful generals as emperors. This phenomenon gave rise to **soldier-emperors**, men chosen by the army in the provinces. Often, a new emperor lasted only a few months or years before being killed in battle or overthrown by another general.

Economic Turmoil

War and civil strife disrupted **trade** and **farming**, leading to shortages and price spikes. The empire tried to mint more coins with less silver to pay soldiers and officials, causing **inflation**. Merchants lost trust in currency, and local barter became common. Wealthy landowners built private defenses, sometimes ignoring imperial tax demands if they could bribe local troops instead.

Taxes rose to fund constant campaigns, burdening ordinary people. Some farmers abandoned their lands, seeking refuge on estates of powerful patrons. Cities shrank or built new walls to protect themselves. This vicious cycle made the empire weaker in meeting outside threats.

Emperors on the Move

From AD 235 to about AD 268, a rapid succession of emperors ruled. Among them:

- **Maximinus Thrax** (AD 235–238): A giant Thracian soldier, he spent his reign campaigning on the frontiers until the Senate backed a revolt that led to his downfall.
- **Gordian III** (AD 238–244): A young emperor, overshadowed by powerful advisors, died during a campaign against the Persians.
- **Philip the Arab** (AD 244–249): Made peace with Persia, but faced new rebellions. Possibly arranged grand celebrations for Rome's 1000th anniversary (AD 248).
- **Decius** (AD 249–251): Fought the Goths, attempted to restore traditional Roman religion by persecuting Christians, but died in battle.
- **Gallus** and **Aemilian** (briefly in AD 251–253): Overthrown by troops.
- **Valerian** (AD 253–260): Captured by the Sassanids, the first Roman emperor to be taken prisoner.
- **Gallienus** (AD 253–268): Co-ruled with Valerian, then alone after his father's capture. He tried reforms but struggled with breakaway empires in Gaul and Palmyra.

In the west, the so-called **Gallic Empire** (AD 260–274) formed under Postumus, who controlled Gaul, Britain, and parts of Spain, acting like a separate Roman state. In the east, **Queen Zenobia** of Palmyra seized power over Syria and Egypt. The central government in Rome was too weak to stop them at first.

Glimmers of Recovery

Despite the chaos, a few strong leaders emerged. **Gallienus** improved the cavalry corps and limited the Senate's role in military commands, hoping to create a more professional officer class. He also supported philosophers and artists in Rome, showing that culture did not vanish even in crisis. But it would take more decisive emperors to reunite the empire.

The Empire on the Brink

By the AD 260s, Rome seemed to be falling apart. The Sassanids loomed in the East, capturing Valerian. The **Gallic Empire** broke away in the West, and in the East, **Palmyra** under Queen Zenobia acted almost as an independent power. Adding to these external and internal divisions, the economy was in freefall, local rebellions erupted, and emperors struggled to pay troops, maintain roads, and protect trade. Some historians call this the empire's near "death experience."

Yet from this chaos, a few energetic emperors arose, determined to reunify the empire. Their success paved the way for deeper reforms under **Diocletian** and later **Constantine**.

Aurelian (AD 270-275)

Restorer of the World

Lucius Domitius Aurelianus—Aurelian—was a capable general chosen by the army. Known for his toughness and speed in battle, he moved swiftly to address threats:

1. **Defeat of the Goths and Vandals**: He secured the Danube frontier, preventing further barbarian incursions into the Balkans.
2. **Recovery of the Palmyrene Empire**: Queen Zenobia had expanded her rule, but Aurelian defeated her forces, capturing Palmyra and restoring Roman control in the East (AD 272).
3. **End of the Gallic Empire**: He negotiated or fought to bring Gaul, Britain, and Spain back under central Roman authority (AD 274).

4. **Aurelian Wall**: In Rome itself, he built a massive new **circuit of walls**, still partially standing today, to protect the capital. This showed that even Rome no longer felt secure without fortifications.

His victories earned him the title **Restitutor Orbis** ("Restorer of the World"). He also introduced a new sun god cult, **Sol Invictus**, hoping to unify religious worship. Unfortunately, he was assassinated by senior officers in AD 275, just as he prepared more campaigns.

The Last Soldier-Emperors Before Diocletian

After Aurelian, several short-lived emperors reigned. Among them:

- **Tacitus** (AD 275-276) and **Probus** (AD 276-282) tried to keep the frontiers stable and encouraged agricultural recovery. **Probus** allowed Germanic settlers to farm in frontier regions under Roman oversight.
- **Carus** (AD 282-283) and his sons, **Carinus** and **Numerian** (AD 283-285), faced internal strife and external threats. In AD 284, the army proclaimed the talented officer **Diocletian** as emperor, overthrowing Carinus.

These men fought constant wars, minted coins, and tried to hold the empire together, but none established a firm government or stable dynasty. The crisis demanded more fundamental solutions.

Diocletian (AD 284-305) and the Road to Recovery

Diocletian was a tough soldier from Dalmatia (roughly modern Croatia). Seizing power in AD 284, he systematically restructured the empire. Though we will explore Diocletian's major reforms in a later chapter, here is a preview of his role in ending the 3rd-century crisis:

1. **Tetrarchy**: He split ruling power among four emperors—two senior **Augusti** and two junior **Caesares**—hoping to guard all frontiers and ensure smooth successions.
2. **Administrative Reforms**: He divided provinces into smaller units and set up new bureaucracies for efficient tax collection.
3. **Edict on Prices**: Attempting to curb inflation, he issued a maximum price list for goods and wages, though enforcement proved difficult.
4. **Military Reorganization**: He separated frontier forces from mobile field armies, better responding to invasions.

By AD 305, Diocletian voluntarily abdicated, leaving a reorganized empire with stronger defenses. Though civil wars followed, the structure he built helped hold Rome together for another century in the West—and much longer in the East.

The Effects of the Crisis on Society

Shift Toward Autocracy

During the crisis, emperors gained more centralized control, relying less on the Senate. Titles like "Dominus" (Lord) became standard, reflecting an increasingly **monarchical** style of rule. The Senate's power dwindled; many senators retreated to their estates. The emperor's court, staffed by military officers and bureaucrats, grew in importance.

Economic Restructuring

To fund constant wars, authorities raised taxes and accepted payments in kind (grain, cattle) if coin was scarce. Local communities became responsible for tax quotas, forcing wealthier residents (curiales) to collect taxes from neighbors and pay deficits themselves. This system tied many city councils to imperial demands. Over time, people sought protection from powerful landowners or joined the army to escape crippling taxes.

Trade still existed, but regions learned to produce what they needed locally, making them less reliant on distant commerce. Craftsmen and peasants were sometimes bound to their occupations to ensure stable production—a step toward medieval "serfdom," though not fully established yet.

Hardships and Change

For ordinary people, these decades were harsh. Raids destroyed farmlands, leading to famine and displacement. Plagues, including the **Cyprian Plague** (possibly smallpox or measles), reduced populations. Fear of invasions forced many to live behind fortified walls. Cultural life persisted—some areas continued building projects or religious shrines—but the atmosphere was anxious.

Christianity spread further during this period, offering communities support and hope, though persecutions under emperors like Decius and Valerian tested believers. Eastern cults, too, gained popularity as people sought spiritual comfort in a dangerous world. The government's official stance on religions could shift dramatically from one emperor to another.

A Glimpse of Hope

Despite the devastation, the empire did not collapse. Military skill and occasional leaders like Aurelian or Diocletian showed that Roman traditions could adapt. Frontier fortresses improved, cavalry units expanded, and the chain of command grew clearer. By AD 300, new power centers (like Trier in Gaul or Nicomedia in Asia Minor) emerged as imperial residences, closer to strategic frontiers than Rome itself.

Roman identity endured, even though some aspects of the classical city-state system faded. This era planted seeds for the **Late Empire**, in which society became more regulated, power more concentrated in the emperor's hands, and Christianity more influential.

Why the Crisis Ended

By the early 4th century, the empire was more regionally governed, with local armies defending each part. The Tetrarchy established by Diocletian, though later unraveling into more civil wars, had introduced the idea that no single person could rule such a vast realm effectively from one city. Over the next chapters, we will see how these changes led to a more divided but still enduring Roman state, especially as the empire formally split between **East** and **West** under later emperors.

CHAPTER 17

REFORMS AND THE LATE EMPIRE

A New Phase of Imperial Rule

In the last chapter, we saw the Roman Empire nearly collapse during the **Crisis of the Third Century** (AD 235–284). Emperors rose and fell quickly, barbarian invasions increased, and the economy suffered severe inflation. Then, a capable general named **Diocletian** took power in AD 284 and introduced major reforms that changed the nature of imperial rule. These reforms, along with those of his successor **Constantine**, shaped what historians call the **Late Empire**.

During this era, the government became more centralized and bureaucratic. Emperors were no longer just "first among equals" but assumed a more royal or divine style. The economy was strictly regulated, and new social rules bound people more closely to their occupations and local communities. Also, Christianity rose from a persecuted minority faith to an officially supported religion, profoundly influencing Roman culture.

Diocletian Takes the Throne (AD 284)

From Soldier to Supreme Ruler

Diocletian was born in Dalmatia (in the western Balkans), of lowly origin. He rose through the army ranks by showing courage and leadership. In AD 284, the army on the eastern frontier proclaimed him emperor after the death of Emperor Numerian. Diocletian defeated another claimant, Carinus, at the Battle of the Margus (AD 285), securing full control of the empire.

After decades of chaos, Diocletian saw that one person could not oversee all borders—from Britain to Egypt, from Spain to Syria—while also handling internal troubles. His solution was the **Tetrarchy**, a shared imperial system.

The Tetrarchy: Rule by Four

Augusti and Caesares

In AD 293, Diocletian appointed a fellow officer, **Maximian**, as co-emperor or **Augustus**, giving him authority over the Western provinces while Diocletian focused on the East. To assist them, Diocletian named **Galerius** as a junior emperor or **Caesar** under himself, and Maximian named **Constantius Chlorus** as Caesar under him.

So the empire had:

1. **Diocletian (Augustus)** in the East.
2. **Maximian (Augustus)** in the West.
3. **Galerius (Caesar)** in the Balkans and Eastern frontiers, under Diocletian.
4. **Constantius Chlorus (Caesar)** in Gaul and Britain, under Maximian.

Each Caesar was expected to succeed his Augustus eventually, ensuring a smooth transition. This system aimed to provide quick responses to threats in any region. Each emperor had his own court and traveled with an army to deal with local troubles.

Splitting Responsibilities

The Tetrarchy led to the creation of new imperial capitals closer to frontier zones. For example, Diocletian resided frequently in **Nicomedia** (in Asia Minor), Maximian in **Mediolanum** (modern

Milan), and so on. Rome remained symbolic as the old capital, but practical governance often took place elsewhere. While this division improved military response, it also widened the gap between the emperor and the traditional senatorial aristocracy in Rome.

Administrative and Economic Reforms

Division into Dioceses and Provinces

To strengthen control and prevent governors from gaining too much power, Diocletian **subdivided provinces**. Smaller provinces, each governed by a praeses or another official, were grouped into **dioceses** under a "vicar" who reported to the central government. This complicated structure gave the empire a large bureaucracy, with numerous officials overseeing taxation, law, and security.

Curiales and Tax System

Collecting taxes was crucial for supporting the large army and bureaucracy. Diocletian continued the trend of making local city council members (called **curiales** or **decurions**) responsible for tax quotas. If people in their district could not pay, the curiales had to cover the shortfall from their own pockets. This was meant to ensure revenues but caused many curiales to resent their role, leading some to flee their cities and seek refuge on estates of powerful landowners.

Edict on Maximum Prices

One famous effort by Diocletian was the **Edict on Maximum Prices** (AD 301). It set a price ceiling on thousands of goods and services—grain, wine, cloth, labor wages, and more—to combat **inflation**, which had soared as coins lost silver content. Violators risked harsh penalties, even death. However, the law was difficult to enforce; merchants hid goods, or people resorted to black-market trading. Eventually, the edict fell into disuse, showing the limits of government control over a vast, diverse economy.

Military Strengthening

Professional Army and Frontier Defense

Diocletian expanded the size of the army, reorganizing it into more mobile field units (comitatenses) and local border garrisons (limitanei). Fortifications were improved along the Rhine, Danube, and eastern frontiers. The Tetrarchy's structure ensured that at least one emperor or Caesar was near each crucial border. This reduced the chance that barbarians or Persian forces could invade unopposed.

Imperial Court Ceremony

To elevate the emperor's status, Diocletian introduced more **elaborate court rituals**. He wore luxurious robes, demanded subjects bow and kiss the hem of his cloak (proskynesis), and used titles like **Dominus** ("Lord") and **Deus** ("God"). This style became known as the **Dominate** (as opposed to the earlier **Principate**). Some Romans found these practices too much like eastern monarchies, but the new ceremony underlined the emperor's authority as almost divine, helping deter conspiracies.

The Great Persecution

Christianity in the Late Third Century

By Diocletian's time, Christianity had spread widely among urban populations, despite periods of persecution under emperors like Decius and Valerian. Christians often formed strong community networks, which some officials feared could undermine loyalty to the traditional gods—and thus the empire's divine protection.

Early in his reign, Diocletian tolerated Christians, focusing on stabilizing the empire. But as he reformed the empire's religion and imposed uniform worship, some advisors and co-rulers (particularly Galerius) saw Christians as a threat. They viewed Christian refusal to sacrifice to pagan gods as disloyal to Rome.

Launching the Persecution

In AD 303, Diocletian issued edicts demanding Christian scriptures be burned, churches destroyed, and Christians who refused to perform sacrifices be punished. This led to a wave of arrests, executions, and forced sacrifices across many provinces. The severity varied by region: in the West, Constantius Chlorus largely ignored the persecution in his territories, while in the East, Galerius enforced it harshly.

The persecution did not crush Christianity. Instead, it created martyrs who inspired even more converts. Eventually, Galerius fell ill and, in AD 311, issued an edict of toleration, admitting that persecuting Christians had not brought success. This shift opened the door for Constantine's later pro-Christian policies.

Diocletian's Abdication

Remarkably, Diocletian retired voluntarily on May 1, AD 305, stepping down at a grand ceremony. He forced Maximian to retire as well, elevating the two Caesars—Galerius and Constantius—to Augusti. Then he withdrew to a palace at **Salona** (in modern Croatia) to tend gardens. He famously refused calls to return to power, saying he preferred growing vegetables in peace.

Unfortunately, Diocletian's Tetrarchy did not remain stable after his departure. Personal ambitions and family ties complicated the succession. When Constantius died in AD 306 in Britain, his son **Constantine** was proclaimed emperor by the army, against the established rules of the Tetrarchy. Meanwhile, Maximian tried to regain power. Soon multiple claimants wrestled for control, leading to another round of civil conflicts.

The Rise of Constantine

Constantine's Path to Power

Constantine was the son of Constantius Chlorus and **Helena**. Born around AD 272/273, he spent time at Diocletian's court, learning imperial politics. After his father's death in AD 306, Constantine's troops in Britain hailed him as Augustus. But Galerius recognized him only as Caesar, giving the rank of Augustus to another. Several emperors vied for power: Galerius, Maxentius, Licinius, and others. Constantine used both diplomacy and military campaigns to strengthen his position. He married his half-sister to Licinius, forming a temporary alliance.

In AD 312, Constantine marched against **Maxentius** (Maximian's son), who controlled Rome and Italy. At the **Battle of the Milvian Bridge** (near Rome), Constantine's forces emerged victorious. Legend says he saw a vision of the Christian symbol (Chi-Rho) and heard the words, "In this sign, conquer," leading him to place Christian symbols on his soldiers' shields.

After Maxentius drowned fleeing the battle, Constantine entered Rome as sole ruler of the Western Empire. He ended the persecution of Christians there and began favoring them with imperial support. Meanwhile, in the East, Licinius gradually became the main Augustus after Galerius's death.

Constantine and Licinius

The Edict of Milan (AD 313)

In AD 313, Constantine and Licinius met in Milan, issuing a joint declaration often called the **Edict of Milan**, granting religious freedom to all and especially legalizing Christianity. This edict returned confiscated Christian property and allowed Christians to worship openly. It did not make Christianity the official state religion yet, but it greatly advanced Christian acceptance.

For a while, Constantine and Licinius ruled as partners, with Constantine in the West and Licinius in the East. But tensions rose.

By AD 324, the two were at war. Constantine defeated Licinius in battles at Adrianople and Chrysopolis, becoming sole emperor of a reunited Roman Empire.

Constantine's Reforms

Founding Constantinople

One of Constantine's most lasting acts was building a new imperial capital on the site of the old Greek city of **Byzantium**, renaming it **Constantinople** (City of Constantine). Dedicated in AD 330, it had strategic advantages: easily defensible, well-located for trade, and near the Danube and eastern frontiers. Constantinople rapidly grew into a major metropolis, symbolizing the East's growing importance.

Rome remained a revered old capital, but Emperors spent little time there. Milan, Trier, and Ravenna also served as Western centers. This shift to Constantinople confirmed the empire's continuing move away from Italy as the sole hub of power.

Administrative Centralization

Constantine continued Diocletian's policies of strong central authority. He reorganized the imperial offices, expanded the palace bureaucracy, and confirmed that local city councils (curiales) were responsible for tax collection. Some laws bound certain professions (like bakers or smiths) to their trades permanently, aiming for stable production.

Monetary Reform: The Solidus

To stabilize the currency, Constantine introduced the **solidus**, a high-quality gold coin that remained a standard for centuries. This helped restore confidence in Roman money, at least for larger transactions, while silver and bronze coins still struggled with inflation. Wealthy elites, especially those in the imperial service or the army, benefited from receiving pay in solidi, but ordinary people often had to manage with lesser coinage.

Constantine and Christianity

The Council of Nicaea (AD 325)

As more Christians gained imperial favor, theological disputes surfaced. One major controversy was **Arianism**, which argued that Jesus was not fully equal to God the Father. To settle this and other issues, Constantine called a council of bishops at **Nicaea** (in modern Turkey) in AD 325. The **Council of Nicaea** produced the **Nicene Creed**, declaring the Father and Son to be of the same divine substance. This set a precedent for imperial involvement in church affairs, shaping Christian theology and unity.

Official Favor

Though Constantine continued some pagan customs and never forced conversion, he built Christian churches, granted privileges to the clergy, and returned confiscated Christian properties. Bishops gained influence in imperial politics, sometimes acting as judges in disputes among Christians. Over time, Christian ethics and Roman law began to intertwine, though pagan worship remained legal until later emperors took stricter measures.

Succession after Constantine

Constantine's Sons

Constantine died in AD 337. He was baptized on his deathbed, sealing his Christian identity. His empire was divided among his three surviving sons—**Constantine II**, **Constans**, and **Constantius II**—leading to internal struggles. By AD 353, Constantius II was sole ruler, continuing Christian support but facing new frontier wars. These family feuds weakened the imperial house and set a pattern of contested successions.

Julian the Apostate (AD 361–363)

A nephew of Constantine, **Julian**, became emperor after Constantius II's death. Raised Christian but influenced by Greek philosophy, he attempted to revive traditional Roman polytheism and reduce Christian privileges—hence later Christians called him "the Apostate." He reformed the empire's administration and led campaigns against the Persians. Julian died in battle in AD 363, ending his short attempt to restore the old gods.

Ongoing Problems in the Late Empire

Even though Diocletian and Constantine had brought stability, challenges remained:

- **Barbarian Pressure**: Germanic tribes like the Goths, Vandals, and Franks kept probing Rome's frontiers. In the East, the Sassanid Persians stayed strong.
- **Economic Burdens**: High taxes and forced services wore down peasants and curiales. Many sought protection from large landowners, eroding central control.
- **Religious Tensions**: While Christianity advanced, disputes between different Christian sects continued, sometimes leading to imperial crackdowns on "heretical" groups.
- **Imperial Succession**: No stable system existed, so civil wars flared. The empire was often divided among co-emperors or relatives, which sometimes worked—but also led to conflict.

In the decades ahead, new emperors tried to balance these issues, culminating in a final official **split** of the empire into East and West under Emperor Theodosius and his successors.

CHAPTER 18

THE SPLIT BETWEEN EAST AND WEST

Two Courts, Two Empires?

We ended the last chapter with **Constantine**'s reforms and the continuing struggle over the frontiers. By the late 4th century AD, pressures from Germanic tribes—like the Goths, Vandals, and others—grew more intense, especially after the Huns pushed these groups westward. Emperors often shared rule among relatives or appointed co-emperors for practical reasons. But after the reign of **Theodosius I**, the empire was formally divided between his two sons, effectively creating a Western Roman Empire and an Eastern Roman Empire.

Theodosius I: Last Emperor of a United Rome

From Spain to the Throne

Theodosius I (AD 379–395) was a skilled general from a Spanish family. After Emperor Valens died at the Battle of Adrianople (AD 378) fighting the Goths, the Eastern Empire was in danger. The Western Emperor **Gratian** appointed Theodosius as co-emperor in the East. Over time, Theodosius regained stability through a mix of warfare and treaties with the Goths, eventually ruling as the sole emperor after the deaths of Western emperors Valentinian II and Eugenius (a usurper).

Thus, Theodosius briefly reunited East and West (AD 394–395), becoming the last man to rule the entire Roman Empire. But the challenges were enormous: barbarian groups roamed the Balkans, the army was short of manpower, and the Western economy was weak.

Official Christianity

Theodosius was a committed Christian. He convened councils (such as the First Council of Constantinople in AD 381) to settle theological disputes and reaffirm the Nicene Creed. He outlawed many pagan practices, closing temples and ending official state pagan rites. By the end of his reign, Christianity was the empire's dominant faith—pagan worship survived in some pockets, but it no longer had state support.

In AD 395, Theodosius died, leaving the empire to his two young sons:

- **Arcadius** in the East (centered in Constantinople).
- **Honorius** in the West (nominally centered in Milan, then Ravenna).

This arrangement was meant to be a shared rulership under one imperial family, but in practice, it led to separate courts and policies.

Permanent Division: East and West

Arcadius and Honorius

Arcadius (AD 395–408) was guided by ministers like Rufinus and later Eudoxia. Honorius (AD 395–423), equally young, relied on powerful generals such as **Stilicho**. The Eastern Empire was wealthier and had more stable frontiers, while the West faced heavier barbarian pressure. Rivalries arose between the courts in Constantinople and Milan (later Ravenna), with each focusing on its own needs.

Many historians mark AD 395 as the formal beginning of the permanent division. From now on, the two halves of the empire had separate imperial lines, though they occasionally cooperated or recognized each other's laws and decrees.

Capitals: Constantinople vs. Ravenna

- **Constantinople (Eastern Capital)**: Prosperous trade routes, strong walls, and a robust treasury. Emperors there could hire mercenaries, maintain armies, and bribe threatening tribes if needed.
- **Ravenna (Western Capital)**: Moved from Milan to Ravenna in AD 402, partly because Ravenna was protected by marshes and the Adriatic Sea. However, it was more isolated, and the West lacked the same tax base and resources as the East. Over time, the Western emperors became heavily dependent on barbarian foederati (allied troops) to defend their territories.

Cultural and Linguistic Divergence

During the 4th century, the empire's linguistic divide sharpened:

- **Latin** remained dominant in the West, used for administration, law, and the army.
- **Greek** was prevalent in the East, especially for local governance, trade, and intellectual life. Over time, Eastern Roman identity grew more Hellenic, while Western Roman identity stayed rooted in Latin traditions.

Religion, too, reflected differences. Both halves were Christian, but theological debates and church leadership often split along cultural lines. Bishops in Constantinople, Alexandria, and Antioch held great sway in the East, while Rome's bishop (the Pope) gained moral authority in the West, though the Eastern emperors recognized the Pope as first among bishops only in an honorary sense.

Barbarian Invasions Intensify

Goths and the Visigoths

The **Goths** were among the first Germanic peoples to form large groups that challenged Rome. Splitting into **Ostrogoths** and **Visigoths**, they had entered Roman territory seeking refuge from the Huns. Mistreatment by local Roman officials led the Visigoths to rebel, resulting in the disastrous **Battle of Adrianople** (AD 378), where Emperor Valens died. Theodosius eventually settled the Visigoths in the Balkans as **foederati**—allowed to live within the empire under their own leaders, in return for military service.

However, tensions never fully went away. By the early 5th century, a Visigoth leader named **Alaric** demanded more land and payment. When the Western government failed to meet his terms, he marched into Italy. In AD 410, the Visigoths **sacked Rome**, an event that shook the Roman world deeply. Though the city's population had declined, Rome still symbolized the empire's eternal power. Its fall to barbarian armies signaled a severe weakness in the West.

Vandals, Suebi, and Others

In late AD 406, a mixed band of Vandals, Suebi, and Alans crossed the frozen Rhine into Gaul. Roman defenses were minimal, and these tribes roamed Gaul, eventually moving into Spain and North Africa. The Vandals, under King Gaiseric, seized Carthage in AD 439, forming a new kingdom. North Africa was a critical source of grain for Italy; its loss crippled the Western Empire's economy.

The Western Empire's Struggle

Honorius, Stilicho, and the Sack of Rome

Honorius was a weak ruler. His talented general **Stilicho** (part Vandal by birth) managed to repel early invasions by Alaric, but political intrigue in the court led to Stilicho's execution in AD 408. With Stilicho gone, the Visigoths found Italy defenseless. Alaric entered Rome, and on August 24, 410, the city was plundered. Though the sack lasted only three days and was relatively controlled by barbarian standards, the psychological impact was huge. Pagan Romans claimed it happened because the gods were abandoned; Christians like St. Augustine wrote works like "City of God" to address those fears.

Britain Abandoned

Roman Britain faced raids from Picts and Scots to the north and Germanic Saxons from the sea. Around AD 410, the Western government could no longer send aid. Honorius reportedly told the Britons to look after their own defense. Roman administration ended in Britain, paving the way for Anglo-Saxon migrations. This was another sign that the West could not protect its distant provinces.

Ravenna's Defense

The swamps around Ravenna made it difficult for large armies to besiege the city, so Western emperors could hide there, even as barbarians roamed Italy. Successive emperors or generals tried to piece together alliances, but the West lacked the strong tax base and resource flow the East had. Over time, local rulers and barbarian warlords carved out separate kingdoms, leaving the Western emperor with little real authority outside Italy.

The Eastern Empire's Different Path

Meanwhile, the **Eastern Empire** under Arcadius and his successors faced tensions—Gothic settlements, the Huns, and religious disputes—but had richer provinces, stable trade routes, and the well-fortified Constantinople. Eastern emperors could often pay off or redirect invaders. They also preserved a more functional bureaucracy and recruited armies from Anatolia and the Balkans.

As a result, the East gradually developed a distinct identity, often called the **Byzantine Empire** by modern historians (though the people themselves still considered it the Roman Empire). This difference would become clearer over time, especially after the West fell in AD 476.

Attempts to Save the West

Aetius and Majorian

Even after 410, the Western Empire did not collapse overnight. Some determined leaders rose:

- **Flavius Aetius** (called "the last of the Romans") was a general who used diplomacy and cunning to handle the Huns, forging alliances with various barbarian groups. He famously defeated Attila the Hun at the Battle of the **Catalaunian Plains** (AD 451) with help from Visigoths and other allies. However, Emperor Valentinian III murdered Aetius in AD 454, losing the West's most capable commander.
- **Majorian** (AD 457–461) tried to restore the empire by building a fleet to challenge the Vandals in North Africa, but internal rivals and the Vandal navy defeated his efforts. Overthrown by the powerful general Ricimer, Majorian's death ended a promising reign.

Rise of Ricimer and Puppet Emperors

Ricimer, a Germanic military leader, dominated Western politics for 15 years. He appointed or deposed emperors at will, effectively ruling behind the throne. Emperors like Libius Severus (AD 461–465) and Anthemius (AD 467–472) were mostly figureheads. Ricimer's focus on personal power prevented the West from uniting against external threats. Meanwhile, barbarian kingdoms grew stronger in Gaul, Spain, and Africa.

The Fall of the Western Empire

Odoacer Deposes Romulus Augustulus (AD 476)

By AD 475, a boy named **Romulus Augustulus** became Western Emperor in name, placed on the throne by his father Orestes. But a Germanic chieftain **Odoacer**, once a Roman officer, led his foederati troops to overthrow Orestes. In AD 476, Odoacer forced Romulus Augustulus to abdicate. Legend says Romulus was allowed to retire peacefully. With that, the Western imperial line ended.

Odoacer did not claim the imperial title; he ruled Italy as a **King**. He sent the imperial regalia to the Eastern Emperor **Zeno**, acknowledging a nominal unity but in reality establishing a post-Roman kingdom in Italy.

Symbolic End

Though life continued, 476 is traditionally marked as the "fall" of the Western Roman Empire. Barbarian kingdoms—Ostrogoths in Italy, Visigoths in Spain, Franks in Gaul, Vandals in Africa—now ruled the former western provinces. Some recognized Eastern emperors or minted coins with their images, but real power lay in local kings. Roman administration, law, and culture blended with Germanic customs to form early medieval societies.

The Eastern Empire (Byzantium) Continues

Survival in the East

In Constantinople, emperors continued unbroken rule for nearly 1,000 more years, though historians refer to them as "Byzantine" from about the 7th century onward. This Eastern Roman Empire preserved Roman law (notably under Emperor Justinian in the 6th century), Greek language, and Christian traditions. It faced challenges from Persians, Arabs, and later Turks, but did not collapse until the fall of Constantinople in AD 1453.

Cultural Legacy

As the East thrived, it maintained many Roman institutions, like the Senate (though it was mostly ceremonial), and the large bureaucratic system inherited from Diocletian and Constantine. Greek became the main language of administration, while Latin faded. Architectural marvels like the **Hagia Sophia** (built under Justinian) showcased a blend of Roman engineering and eastern influences. Scholars in Constantinople preserved and copied ancient texts, passing on Greek and Roman knowledge to future generations.

Differences Set in Stone

By the late 5th century, the division was permanent: a Latin-based, fractured West ruled by barbarian kings and an Eastern empire in Constantinople continuing the Roman name and tradition. Church leadership also diverged, with the Pope in Rome and the Patriarch in Constantinople sometimes agreeing, sometimes arguing over doctrines and authority.

Over time, Western Europe entered the early Middle Ages—often called the "Dark Ages" in older histories, though modern scholars note there was still learning and culture, just differently organized. Meanwhile, the Eastern Empire (Byzantine) developed a rich Christian civilization, blending Roman law and Greek heritage.

Chapter 18 Summary

1. **Theodosius I (AD 379–395):** The last emperor to rule a united Roman Empire. He made Nicene Christianity the official doctrine, took measures against paganism, and after his death, the empire split between his sons Arcadius (East) and Honorius (West).
2. **Separate Courts and Capitals:** Constantinople became the rich, well-defended seat of the Eastern Empire, while Ravenna became the Western capital—marshy but safer than Milan. Language and culture diverged: Greek dominated in the East, Latin remained in the West.
3. **Barbarian Invasions:** Visigoths, Vandals, and other groups crossed into Roman lands. In AD 410, Alaric's Visigoths sacked Rome; in AD 439, Vandals seized Carthage. The West lost vital resources.
4. **Struggles in the West:** Leaders like Stilicho, Aetius, and Majorian attempted to defend the Western Empire, but court intrigue and lack of resources hampered them. Barbarian kingdoms emerged in Gaul, Spain, and Africa.

5. **Fall of the Western Empire (AD 476):** Odoacer deposed Romulus Augustulus, ending the imperial line in the West. New kingdoms replaced Roman rule, blending Roman and Germanic traditions.
6. **Eastern (Byzantine) Empire Continues:** In Constantinople, emperors ruled for centuries more, preserving Roman law, Christian religion, and Greek culture. The East's relative wealth and strong defense allowed it to survive.

CHAPTER 19

THE FALL OF THE WESTERN EMPIRE

The Final Days of Western Rome

In **Chapter 18**, we saw how the Roman Empire was officially split into an Eastern half (ruled from Constantinople) and a Western half (often ruled from Ravenna). The Eastern Empire fared better, thanks to stronger finances and well-defended borders. The West, however, struggled against heavy **barbarian invasions**, weak leadership, and a crumbling economy. In AD 476, the last Western emperor was deposed by a Germanic king, marking what many historians call the "fall" of the Western Roman Empire.

This chapter explores how the West stumbled from crisis to crisis, losing key provinces to barbarian groups. We will see the role of men like **Aetius**, **Majorian**, and the powerful general **Ricimer**, who tried to hold things together or used the turmoil for personal gain. We will also focus on the final puppet emperors, the sacks of Rome, and the dramatic moment when the West's last emperor lost his throne.

Western Rome After AD 410

The Shattered Heartland

When the Visigoths left Italy in AD 412, they moved into southern Gaul and later into Spain, where they settled as **foederati** under limited Roman authority. Italy itself was exhausted, farmland ruined, and morale broken. The Western Emperor **Honorius** remained in Ravenna, heavily reliant on his general **Stilicho**'s memory (though Stilicho had already been executed in AD 408) and subsequent advisers.

Roman Britain, left undefended, had declared its own local leaders. Over the next few years, the provinces in Gaul and Spain were constantly raided or occupied by Vandals, Suebi, and Alans. Many local Romans tried to strike deals with these newcomers, who established small kingdoms or roaming warbands.

The Rise of Competent Generals

Some Western leaders tried to salvage the situation:

1. **Constantius III**: Married Honorius's sister, Galla Placidia. He momentarily stabilized the situation in Italy and forced the Visigoths to accept land in southern Gaul.
2. **Placidia's Influence**: Galla Placidia, a strong-willed princess, became mother and regent to the future emperor **Valentinian III** (AD 425–455). She guided Western policy with the help of generals and administrators, though conditions kept deteriorating.

When Constantius III died, new troubles emerged, and the Western army had fewer and fewer Roman-born troops, relying on barbarian allies or mercenaries. The strong men who led the West's armies had to juggle the demands of the court in Ravenna, their barbarian soldiers, and unstoppable outside threats.

Threats from New Directions

The Huns Appear

The **Huns**, fierce horsemen from Central Asia, had driven the Goths into Roman lands decades earlier. By the mid-5th century, a charismatic Hun leader named **Attila** rose to command a large confederation of tribes. Nicknamed the "Scourge of God" by some Romans, Attila invaded both Eastern and Western territories, looting cities and forcing emperors to pay large sums in gold.

While the Eastern Empire paid Attila off to stay out of Constantinople, the West found itself less capable of paying or defending. In AD 451, Attila marched into Gaul, where a combined force of Romans (led by Aetius) and Visigoths confronted him at the **Battle of the Catalaunian Plains**. Attila was forced to withdraw, marking a significant (though temporary) Western victory.

Burgundians and Others

Many smaller groups, like the **Burgundians**, settled within the western provinces. Some founded local kingdoms, such as the Burgundian Kingdom in southeastern Gaul. Roman officials tried to create treaties (*foedera*) that gave these groups land in exchange for military service. This policy sometimes slowed invasions but also carved up the empire into semi-independent regions, reducing Ravenna's direct control.

Aetius: The "Last of the Romans"

His Rise to Power

Flavius Aetius (AD 396–454) is often called the "last of the Romans" for his attempts to defend the Western Empire. Of mixed Roman and barbarian background, Aetius had lived among the Huns in his youth as a diplomatic hostage. He used his knowledge of their ways to build alliances and secure the West's frontiers as best he could. By AD 433, he became the dominant general under Emperor **Valentinian III**, overshadowing the weak court in Ravenna.

Saving Gaul from Attila

When Attila invaded Gaul in AD 451, Aetius formed an alliance with the Visigothic king Theodoric I. Their combined army met the Huns at the **Battle of the Catalaunian Plains**. This battle was brutal, but

Attila failed to defeat the Romans and Goths. He withdrew, later invading Italy in AD 452 but turning back after failing to capture major cities—perhaps due to disease or lack of supplies. While Aetius did not eradicate the Hun threat, he prevented a total disaster in Gaul and Italy.

Betrayal in AD 454

Despite Aetius's success, Emperor Valentinian III grew suspicious of his powerful general. Fearing Aetius might seize the throne, Valentinian invited him to a meeting and murdered him personally, aided by guards. The Western court lost its most capable protector, leaving no strong figure to handle the next wave of crises.

Majorian: A Brief Glimmer of Hope

The Short Reign of a Skilled Emperor (AD 457–461)

After Valentinian III's assassination in AD 455, power struggles ensued. Eventually, a general named **Majorian** rose to the throne in AD 457. He showed remarkable energy and intelligence for a Western emperor at this late stage. Majorian tried to reorganize the army, strengthen fortifications in Gaul, and even planned to reconquer North Africa from the Vandals, who had established a powerful kingdom in Carthage.

However, Majorian's fleet was destroyed by the Vandals before it could sail. He returned to Italy to find that his leading general, **Ricimer**, turned against him. Ricimer forced Majorian to abdicate and then had him executed in AD 461. The West lost a promising leader who might have turned things around. Instead, it fell further under the control of strong generals who effectively chose puppet emperors.

The Sack of Rome by the Vandals (AD 455)

The Vandal Kingdom in North Africa

Years earlier, the Vandals had crossed from Spain into North Africa under King **Gaiseric**. By AD 439, they took Carthage, capturing Rome's richest grain-producing lands. From this base, Vandal ships raided the Mediterranean coast. Gaiseric aimed to build a maritime empire, attacking Roman towns in Sicily, Sardinia, and Corsica.

The Second Sack of Rome

In AD 455, after Valentinian III was killed, Gaiseric saw an opportunity. He sailed a fleet to the mouth of the Tiber and approached Rome. The new Western government, weakened by internal power struggles, could not mount a defense. Over two weeks, the Vandals looted the city. While not as catastrophic as some legends suggest, they took enormous wealth, including precious statues, gold, and possibly the treasures brought from Jerusalem centuries earlier by Titus. They also captured many Romans as slaves.

Unlike the short Visigothic sack in 410, the Vandals' thorough plundering gave rise to the modern word "vandalism"—destruction or defacement of property. For the Western Empire, the event further wrecked morale and displayed Rome's helplessness against maritime raids. Though the city still had people living in it, its old splendor was fading.

Consequences for the Western Empire

Economic Collapse

With North Africa gone, Italy no longer received regular grain shipments. Tax revenues fell sharply. Much farmland in Gaul, Spain, and Britain was under barbarian control. Italian estates were short on workers and faced repeated invasions that destroyed crops. The West's treasury lacked funds to maintain a strong field army or pay off enemies, leading to reliance on local warlords and half-hearted allies.

Barbarian Kingdoms Grow

The Visigoths in southwestern Gaul and most of Spain, the Burgundians in southeastern Gaul, the Franks in northern Gaul, and the Vandals in Africa all expanded. Each had its own king, laws, and treaties with Rome. Officially, they recognized the Western emperor in some form, but in practice, they ruled independently. Roman officials in these regions often adapted by cooperating with local barbarian rulers, merging Roman and Germanic traditions.

Ravenna Under Strong Generals

Emperors like **Libius Severus** (AD 461–465) and **Anthemius** (AD 467–472) were largely controlled by Ricimer, the powerful Germanic general who acted as "kingmaker." He married into the imperial family at times, then turned against emperors he disliked. This state of affairs continued until Ricimer's death in AD 472, but the cycle persisted with other generals who took his place.

At this point, the West was a patchwork of nominally Roman territories and barbarian kingdoms. The Eastern Emperor in Constantinople sometimes tried to intervene, sending a candidate emperor or an expedition against the Vandals. But the East had its own priorities, and the West's decline continued.

The Last Emperors (AD 455–476)

Ricimer's Puppet Emperors

From AD 455 onward, a series of weak Western emperors came and went under the influence of Ricimer or other strong generals:

- **Avitus** (455–456): A Gallic noble. Deposed by Ricimer after failing to stop the Vandals.
- **Majorian** (457–461): A capable reformer, toppled by Ricimer.
- **Libius Severus** (461–465): Little is known; died in office, likely manipulated by Ricimer.
- **Anthemius** (467–472): Sent from Constantinople as a bridge between East and West. Failed in a campaign against the Vandals. Killed in a civil war with Ricimer.
- **Olybrius** (472): Placed by Ricimer, died shortly after Ricimer himself.
- **Glycerius** (473–474): Largely unknown, overshadowed by a new challenger from the East.

- **Julius Nepos** (474–475 in Italy, recognized until 480 in Dalmatia): Sent by the Eastern emperor Leo I. Nepos was overthrown by his general, Orestes, who installed his own son as emperor.

Romulus Augustulus (AD 475–476)

The final Western emperor was a teenage boy ironically named **Romulus Augustulus**. His father, **Orestes**, a former secretary to Attila the Hun, made him emperor in late AD 475. Romulus Augustulus had no real power; the real authority lay with Orestes.

Yet events moved swiftly. A group of foederati in Italy, under the leadership of **Odoacer**, demanded land in Italy as a reward for service. Orestes refused, prompting them to revolt. In AD 476, Orestes was killed, and Odoacer marched on Ravenna. There, he deposed Romulus Augustulus. Out of pity, Odoacer spared the young ex-emperor, granting him a pension and letting him live quietly, though he was never a threat again.

With Romulus gone, no new Western emperor was named. Odoacer presented himself as King of Italy and sent the imperial insignia to the Eastern Emperor **Zeno**, claiming there was no need for a separate Western emperor. This symbolic act marks the traditional end of the Western Roman Empire.

Aftermath in Italy

Odoacer's Rule (AD 476–493)

Odoacer governed Italy with a mix of Roman administration and barbarian customs. He maintained relations with the Senate and minted coins in the name of the Eastern Emperor. Many Romans in Italy accepted his rule, relieved to have some stability after years of puppet emperors. Still, Odoacer's power was limited by other barbarian nations. In AD 493, the Ostrogothic king **Theoderic** defeated Odoacer, creating an Ostrogothic Kingdom in Italy that preserved some Roman traditions for a time.

Theoderic the Great

The **Ostrogoths**, another branch of the Gothic people, had been foederati in the Balkans. Invited by Emperor Zeno to remove Odoacer, Theoderic entered Italy, overcame Odoacer, and ruled from Ravenna. He respected Roman laws, worked with the Senate, and tried to keep peace among Ostrogoths and Romans. This state (AD 493–553) was one of several "successor kingdoms," blending Roman governance with Germanic leadership. Though not part of the Roman Empire officially, it carried on many Roman ways.

Outside Italy: Barbarian Kingdoms

By the late 5th century, Western Europe was dotted with new realms:

- **Visigothic Kingdom** in Aquitaine (Gaul) and much of Spain, eventually moving its capital to Toledo.
- **Burgundian Kingdom** in southeastern Gaul.
- **Frankish Kingdom** in northern Gaul, led by **Clovis**, who would convert to Christianity around AD 496, forging a powerful dynasty.
- **Vandal Kingdom** in North Africa, harassing Mediterranean shipping until the Eastern Emperor Justinian reconquered it in the 6th century.
- **Suebi** in part of northwestern Spain, though overshadowed by the Visigoths.

These new powers recognized some Roman titles or formed alliances with local Roman elites. Over time, Roman culture, language, and law intertwined with Germanic customs, shaping what we call **medieval Europe**.

Why Did the West Fall?

Historians debate the causes. Likely it was a mix of:

1. **Military Shortcomings**: Reliance on barbarian foederati and the shrinking core of Roman legions.
2. **Economic Weakness**: Loss of tax-rich provinces like Africa, farmland devastation, inflation, and failing trade networks.
3. **Political Instability**: Frequent coups, puppet emperors, and powerful warlords more concerned with personal gain than unity.
4. **Barbarian Invasions**: Large-scale migrations pressed from all directions, forcing the empire to grant land to groups who became independent.
5. **Eastern Neglect**: The East survived, but it often left the West to fend for itself.

No single factor sealed the West's fate, but all combined to erode its capacity to function. The official end in AD 476 merely confirmed a reality that had existed for decades: the Western empire was fragmented beyond repair.

Life Goes On

Although the Roman imperial structure in the West ended, Roman traditions did not vanish overnight. Many barbarians admired Roman law, Christianity, and city life. They kept Roman taxes, coinage, and, in some cases, the Latin language. Over centuries, new forms of governance blended Roman and Germanic elements, giving birth to the early medieval kingdoms.

Even the Senate in Rome lingered for a while, though it had little real power. The Pope in Rome started gaining more influence in religious matters and, eventually, in political affairs. Monasteries kept some classical learning alive. Meanwhile, the Eastern Empire (Byzantine) thrived, preserving a direct continuation of Roman governance for almost another thousand years.

CHAPTER 20

ROME'S LEGACY THROUGH LATE ANTIQUITY

Rome's Enduring Influence

We have traced Rome's rise from a small settlement to a vast empire, its transformation under emperors, the crisis of the third century, and the eventual split. Finally, we saw the Western Empire collapse in AD 476, replaced by barbarian kingdoms. However, **Rome's legacy** did not vanish. Its impact on language, law, architecture, religion, and governance stretched far beyond the empire's official fall. Even in the lands of the new barbarian rulers, Roman ideas merged with local customs, creating the foundation of medieval European culture. Meanwhile, in the East, the Byzantine Empire carried on Roman law and traditions for almost a millennium more.

The Byzantine Empire: Rome Lives On in the East

Lasting Roman State

After the West fell in AD 476, the Eastern Roman Empire (called "Byzantine" by modern historians) remained. Emperors in Constantinople continued to see themselves as the rightful Roman rulers. Indeed, they often tried to reconquer lost territories in the West:

- **Emperor Justinian** (AD 527–565) famously sent armies under General **Belisarius** to reclaim North Africa from the Vandals, Italy from the Ostrogoths, and parts of Spain from the Visigoths. He succeeded temporarily, although these gains were hard to keep.

- Byzantines preserved Roman law in Justinian's **Corpus Juris Civilis** (Body of Civil Law), a major collection of legal texts including the **Codex**, **Digest**, **Institutes**, and later the **Novels**.

The city of **Constantinople**—protected by massive walls built under Theodosius II—became a thriving center of trade and culture. While it increasingly used Greek language, the imperial government still called itself "Roman," and the emperors considered themselves successors to Augustus and Constantine. As centuries passed, this Eastern state blended classical Roman governance with Christian and Hellenic influences, forming a unique civilization that lasted until AD 1453.

Christian Powerhouse

Byzantine emperors saw themselves as defenders of **Orthodox Christianity**. The Patriarch of Constantinople rivaled the Pope in Rome as a major church leader. Councils met in the East to resolve theological disputes—such as **Chalcedon** (AD 451) and later synods. This strong church-state relationship shaped Byzantine culture deeply. Monasteries preserved ancient manuscripts, while theologians debated doctrines that influenced both Eastern and Western Christianity.

Roman Law's Enduring Impact

The Legacy of Roman Legal Codes

Though the Western Empire faded, Roman law did not. Many barbarian kings and local rulers found Roman legal principles practical for governing mixed Roman-barbarian populations. They issued codes inspired by Roman law, such as the **Lex Visigothorum** (Visigothic Code) and the **Burgundian Code**, combining Roman jurisprudence with Germanic traditions.

In the East, Justinian's **Corpus Juris Civilis** became the authoritative statement of Roman law. It organized centuries of legislation and juristic writings, making them easier to use. Even after Justinian's reconquests faded, his law code remained influential:

1. **In Byzantium**, it evolved over centuries, guiding the empire's legal system.
2. **In Western Europe**, medieval scholars rediscovered it around the 11th century at universities like Bologna, shaping the development of Canon Law (church law) and modern civil law traditions.
3. **In Modern Times**, many legal systems around the world still carry concepts from Roman law, like contracts, property rights, and legal procedures.

Practical Effects

Roman law introduced principles such as:

- **Innocent until proven guilty** (though not formally stated in those exact words, the idea emerged from Roman legal debates).
- **Burden of proof** on the accuser.
- Clear definitions of wills, inheritance, property, and contractual obligations.

Even in the chaotic early medieval West, some cities kept small law courts that followed local Roman practices, especially in southern Gaul or parts of Italy. Over time, new rulers recognized that adopting Roman law gave them legitimacy among local Roman populations.

The Christian Church and Rome's Influence

Organizational Structure

Rome's administrative style influenced the Christian Church. Bishops governed local dioceses, similar to how Roman officials governed provinces. The Church borrowed Roman titles (like pontifex maximus, once used by emperors) and adapted them into Christian contexts. Over centuries, the Western Church, led by the Pope (bishop of Rome), claimed special authority because Rome had been the empire's spiritual capital from the time of the apostles Peter and Paul.

Monasticism and Scholarship

Monasteries, starting with figures like **St. Benedict** (late 5th–early 6th century), became centers of learning, preserving ancient texts. Monks copied manuscripts, including Roman authors like Virgil, Cicero, and Ovid, alongside Christian writings. This allowed Roman literature, philosophy, and historical records to survive through the Middle Ages. Without these copying efforts, much of our knowledge of classical Rome would have been lost.

Political Power of the Papacy

As the Western Empire disintegrated, the Pope in Rome became more influential. Local rulers in Italy and beyond sometimes sought papal blessings to strengthen their legitimacy. For instance, the Frankish king **Pepin the Short** and later **Charlemagne** allied with popes, creating the "Carolingian Empire." The Church's moral and social influence helped shape Europe's political landscape well into the medieval period.

Latin and the Romance Languages

Latin's Transformation

During the empire, **Latin** was the official language in the West, used for law, administration, and the army. As the empire declined in the West, Vulgar Latin (the everyday spoken form) varied from region to region. Over centuries, these differences grew into distinct **Romance languages**, such as:

- **Italian** in the Italian Peninsula.
- **French** in Gaul.
- **Spanish** in Hispania.
- **Portuguese** in Lusitania (western Iberia).
- **Romanian** in the former province of Dacia and surrounding areas.

Classical Latin remained in use for church services, scholarly writing, and official documents, especially in the Catholic Church. Medieval monks, bishops, and kings still wrote Latin letters or kept Latin records. This continuity ensured that educated Europeans across different kingdoms could communicate in Latin, fostering cultural unity. Eventually, each region's vernacular (spoken language) diverged more, but the common Latin root gave them shared vocabulary and structures.

Literature and Learning

Roman literature was preserved by Christian scribes who admired certain classical texts for their style or moral lessons. Even as the empire fragmented, some schools taught grammar, rhetoric, and basic arithmetic, passing on a simplified version of Roman education. Writers like **Boethius** (early 6th century) and **Cassiodorus** (also 6th century) tried to bridge classical knowledge and Christian faith, influencing medieval scholarship.

Architecture and Infrastructure

Roman Building Techniques

Roman architecture—a hallmark of the empire—did not vanish with the Western collapse. New rulers admired Roman roads, aqueducts, arches, and concrete. They reused old structures or built new ones influenced by Roman models. For example:

- **Arches and Vaults**: Medieval churches in Europe often employed round arches reminiscent of Roman basilicas.
- **Reused Stones**: Barbarian kings or local communities frequently scavenged stone from old Roman monuments to build fortifications or churches. This practice, called **spoliation**, allowed Roman masonry to live on in medieval walls and cathedrals.
- **Roads**: Many Roman roads remained in use for centuries, guiding trade routes and pilgrimages. They formed the backbone of European travel networks.

Roman cities served as centers for bishops and local counts, even if many neighborhoods fell into ruin. The Roman forum might become a marketplace, and old temples might be converted into churches or left as quarries for building materials.

Public Works Inspiration

Byzantine architecture, especially under Emperor Justinian (e.g., the Hagia Sophia), built upon Roman engineering knowledge, adding creative dome techniques. In the West, the concept of massive public works slowed due to war and poverty, but smaller-scale projects kept some Roman styles alive. Later medieval engineers studied Roman ruins to learn about arches, domes, and water supply systems.

The Symbolic Power of Rome

Roman Titles and Claims

Throughout the Middle Ages, rulers sought the prestige of Roman heritage. The idea of a "Roman Empire" in the West resurfaced when the Pope crowned **Charlemagne** as "Emperor of the Romans" on Christmas Day, AD 800. This event aimed to revive an image of Roman unity and glory, though Charlemagne's empire was more of a Frankish-led Christian realm. Later, the "Holy Roman Empire" in the German lands likewise claimed to continue Roman imperial tradition, though it differed greatly from ancient Rome.

Christian "Rome" as an Ideal

Even as real political power dwindled in the city of Rome, it remained the seat of the Pope, giving it spiritual significance. Pilgrims visited the tombs of saints Peter and Paul, linking their faith to ancient Rome's apostolic tradition. The city's name carried weight in matters of religious authority. Eastern emperors in Constantinople also preserved the name "Roman." Their subjects often called themselves "Rhomaioi" (Romans in Greek).

Thus, "Rome" remained a powerful word, standing for imperial legitimacy, Christian heritage, and civilized order, long after the empire's physical might was gone.

Looking Beyond the Fall

The Transition into the Middle Ages

Modern scholars sometimes call the period from around AD 300 to 600 "Late Antiquity," stressing continuity rather than abrupt change. In the West, the political structures changed drastically, but many day-to-day aspects (laws, languages, city life) evolved slowly. Over centuries, Germanic, Celtic, and Roman elements merged into early medieval cultures. The East (Byzantine Empire) maintained more direct Roman traditions, preserving literacy, urban life, and classical scholarship.

Lasting Achievements

1. **Law**: Roman concepts form the foundation of many modern legal systems, especially in Europe and Latin America.
2. **Language**: Latin gave birth to Romance languages and remained the language of scholarship for centuries.
3. **Architecture**: Arches, aqueducts, roads, and building styles influenced medieval, Renaissance, and even modern construction.
4. **Religion**: The Christian Church structured itself much like the Roman administration. Popes and bishops inherited many aspects of Roman governance.
5. **Cultural Identity**: The idea of "being Roman" lingered in the East until 1453 and in the West through the Holy Roman Empire and various monarchies claiming Roman descent.

Rome's Ongoing Legacy

Even today, we use the Roman alphabet (with modifications) for many Western languages. Our modern law codes draw on Roman legal principles. Latin terms like **et cetera (etc.), versus (vs.)**, and **status quo** remain in daily use. Architecture still employs arches and domes perfected by Roman engineers. Many Christian denominations trace spiritual and organizational roots to the early Church shaped by Roman structures.

For over **two thousand years**, the influence of Rome has touched literature, government, religion, and culture. While no empire lasts forever, Rome's contributions continue to shape societies worldwide. The story of Rome—its **rise**, **unprecedented achievements**, **struggles**, and **transformation**—remains one of history's most impressive arcs, a testament to both human creativity and the challenges that come with great power.

Conclusion: The Spirit of Rome

As we close our book, we see that **Rome** never truly "disappeared." It evolved. The Western Empire fell in AD 476, but Roman law, language, and customs lived on in new kingdoms and the Catholic Church. The Eastern (Byzantine) Empire carried the Roman torch until AD 1453. Over the centuries, leaders across Europe claimed Roman titles to legitimize their power. Scholars revived classical learning in the Renaissance, calling themselves "humanists," once again seeking wisdom from Roman texts.

Rome's story is about city dwellers along the Tiber forging a kingdom, a republic, and then an empire so large that it shaped all future Western civilizations. It is a tale of courage, innovation, but also internal strife and eventual decline. Yet through it all, Rome left a permanent imprint on laws, languages, religions, and architecture. Whenever we speak a Romance language, study law, read Latin phrases, or admire a domed building, we remember that *all roads truly did lead to Rome.*

Help Us Share Your Thoughts!

Dear reader,

Thank you for spending your time with this book. We hope it brought you enjoyment and a few new ideas to think about. If there was anything that didn't work for you, or if you have suggestions on how we can improve, please let us know at **kontakt@skriuwer.com**. Your feedback means a lot to us and helps us make our books even better.

If you enjoyed this book, we would be very grateful if you left a review on the site where you purchased it. Your review not only helps other readers find our books, but also encourages us to keep creating more stories and materials that you'll love.

By choosing Skriuwer, you're also supporting **Frisian**—a minority language mainly spoken in the northern Netherlands. Although **Frisian** has a rich history, the number of speakers is shrinking, and it's at risk of dying out. Your purchase helps fund resources to preserve and promote this language, such as educational programs and learning tools. If you'd like to learn more about Frisian or even start learning it yourself, please visit **www.learnfrisian.com**.

Thank you for being part of our community. We look forward to sharing more books with you in the future.

Warm regards,
The Skriuwer Team

www.ingramcontent.com/pod-product-compliance
Lightning Source LLC
LaVergne TN
LVHW012041070526
838202LV00056B/5557